A Kentucky Sharecropper's Struggles:

The Lives of Paul & Rosa Clark

A Kentucky Sharecropper's Struggles:

The Lives of Paul & Rosa Clark

by Norbert Clark

Cover photo: The Jim Smallwood farm where Paul and
Rosie Clark lived in 1943-1944.

Cover and other landscape photos by Norbert Clark
Additional Clark photographs from family collection.

Printed in the United States of America

ISBN-13: 9781501002700

ISBN-10: 1501002708

Editing and design and publication arrangements
by Sara E. Leeland, Holland, Michigan

Table of Contents

MORE HISTORY AND GENEOLOGY
OF THE CLARK & MILLINER FAMILIES

NOTE TO READERS

MAPS SHOWING LOCATION OF FARMS
AND OTHER PLACES NOTED IN BOOK

Two hand-drawn maps, followed by descriptions of the places are included with picture on pages 106-107. Both the maps and descriptions show the Kentucky farms that Paul and Rosie Clark rented and on which they lived and worked. The list ends with the farm that Paul and Rosie were able to purchase. The maps also show places described in the book: the Johnson School, St. Paul's Church and School, the roads of the immediate area, and the some of the places named, like 'Tood's Ford' and 'Joe Langley's Beehive.'

INTRODUCTION

This book was written as a description of the happy but difficult lives of my parents, Joseph Paul Clark (1912-1964) and Rosa Catherine Milliner Clark (1914-1952), who married in Kentucky in 1932. Rosie and Paul were subsistence farmers in West-Central Kentucky where family incomes depended on the basic skills of farming, gardening, hunting, fishing, making whiskey and growing tobacco.

Paul and Rosie learned these skills. Like their parents and grandparents, they attended the one-room schools. They travelled the one-track dirt roads in their horse-drawn farm wagons, fording the creeks through the shallow riffles. They farmed the rough steep hill lands with the horses and mules, using the same tools their parents and grandparents had used in the 1800s.

Rosie and Paul's short lives transitioned difficult times. The tobacco market which was the main source of income for these small farmers failed completely in the 1920s. Then Prohibition outlawed the production and sale of whiskey, a major source of income for the Milliner family.

Although Paul and Rosie's life together started with a minimum of education and was interrupted by the depression, a flood and a war, they lived comfortably together for two decades. Rosie, as the oldest of nine children had a positive attitude and the maturity to take responsibility—strong stabilizing factors for the family. Paul, who had been taken out of school in the sixth grade to help support his family, had experience in facing and solving life's struggles. Rosie gave birth to eight healthy children. Paul worked as a sharecropper on the farms where they lived daily from dawn to dusk. Their day-to-day lives were happy and unstressed.

Paul had learned to play the fiddle as a boy. He earned a few extra dollars playing music for the local square dances held in the neighbors' homes. He entertained the family, all of whom learned to appreciate music. The younger children danced and jigged when Paul played the fiddle and reveled in their ability to entertain the family. The dawn-to-dusk responsibilities and hard labor were interrupted by these moments of relaxation and entertainment.

Paul cooperated with their neighbors, sharing hard jobs like harvesting hay or corn fodder, and setting, cutting and stripping tobacco, or harvesting timber and building a crib or a barn. He looked forward to the day when he could own a farm or buy a tractor. He sometimes rented extra land and worked extra hard to achieve these goals. Still, the progress was slow because, as a sharecropper a third of the produce was owed to the land owner.

Rosie managed the house, the garden, the chickens and the children. She sewed most of their clothes: the shirts, the dresses and even the underwear, everything except the heavy Duckhead denim work overalls worn by Paul and the older boys. She took responsibility for the weekly washing and ironing and the weekly baths in the wash tub. She cooked three meals each day, managing without electricity or refrigeration, and each meal was fresh and tasty, whether from the garden or the cellar. The menus were dictated by the meats in the smokehouse, the vegetables and fruits in the garden and the orchard, or the cans of vegetables and fruits in the cellar.

Much of the work was shared. Paul built the fires first thing in the morning while Rosie clothed the children. The cook stove would then be hot so Rosie could cook the breakfast while Paul and the older boys went to the barn to milk the cows and feed the horses for work in the fields. Sharing the work and the recreation played a major role in their lives.

Church and prayer also played a major role. The family attended Sunday Mass, making the trip with horses and farm wagon when possible. In bad weather, or when the children were small, Paul rode the horse to Church. Bedtime prayers and grace before meals were mandatory. The children memorized standard prayers and the family recited the rosary together most nights.

Paul and Rosie maintained long friendships and had the deep respect of their neighbors. They had attended school with many of these friends. Paul, playing music and sharing work with the neighbors, was considered a prominent member of the community. Rosie, with her healthy family, her jolly and skilled participation and her generous contribution of tasty food for funerals and wedding dinners, was closely involved with the larger community.

Through their struggles and set-backs, they maintained a positive attitude. They were considered a necessary part of the community. When they died, suddenly and prematurely, Rosie at 38 years of age and Paul at 52 years, the community as well as the family was devastated.

As Paul and Rosie's oldest son, I shared and remember much of their life together. Although anyone interested in the history of Kentucky in the 20th century may enjoy this book, my main objective in writing is to instill in Paul and Rosie's grandchildren and great-grandchildren the same respect and admiration for them that I have. I hope that I can be half as successful with the task as my parents were with their lives

PAUL AND ROSIE'S SONG

A sharecropper's life means moving often

To a new farm down the road.

Well I wonder; yes I wonder;

Can we carry this heavy load?

Lord, please smooth this bumpy road.

Loaded up to move this morning,

Horses ate their corn and hay.

Well I wonder; yes I wonder;

Will these sunny skies turn gray?

Will dark catch us on the way?

The wagon creaks; the horses strain;

The clouds above, they look like rain.

Well I wonder; yes I wonder;

Will we pass this way again?

Send the sunshine with the rain.

The house is small, the bushes taller;

The hills are rough and filled with stone.

Well I wonder what is yonder;

Can it be that pot of gold?

Life is filled with wealth untold.

Beans, potatoes, corn, tomatoes,

A mule to plow these rocky hills.

Well I wonder; yes I wonder;

Can we work and pay the bills?

Lord, deliver us from ills.

Loaded up to move this morning;

Down the road we go again.

Well I wonder - what is yonder?

Came my loved one's soft refrain,

Will we pass this way again?

Came my loved one's soft refrain,

Send the sunshine with the rain.

Came my loved one's soft refrain,

Nothing ventured, nothing gained!

--Song by Norbert Clark

Acknowledgements

- To my wife, Karen, whose encouragement and typing skills accelerated the project

- To my cousin, Cathy Blass, who supplied most of the genealogical information and shared my interest in history and family

- To my brothers and sisters who filled in gaps in the family stories

- To my parents, grandparents and relatives who repeated the stories many times

- To editor Sara Leeland for her encouragement and advice on content

1
ROSIE

Born in a Log Cabin

Rosa (always called 'Rosie') was the first child born in 1914 to Edward and Mary Alta Milliner.* As a young married couple, Edward and Mary Alta had moved into a log cabin by a fresh water spring on a north hillside of the old Milliner farm in Grayson County, Kentucky. According to Rosie, the Milliner land was an allotment to family who had fought in the Revolutionary War. Both George Washington and Thomas Jefferson also owned land in Grayson and the adjoining counties.

Rosie, like her mother, had completed the eighth grade at the one-room Johnson School. Her father, Edward, had not attended school. He could neither read nor write, and he valued work experience over school education. Rosie's mother, Mary Alta, was also a Milliner and a distant cousin of Edward's. She had attended Johnson Public School through the eighth grade. She read incessantly, and encouraged her children to get an education.

---

*The historical spelling of the name Milliner is diverse. Miller, Milner, and Milliner can be found in the records. The most common spelling in the early 1800s was Milner.

Learning Traditional Survival Skills

Rosie grew up in an atmosphere of 24-hour a day activity. At an early age, she had helped her father in the fields, learning from him how to work the mules, cultivate the crops, hoe the corn and tobacco, and both kill and process the hogs. Eventually, she learned how to manage the farm, the garden and the livestock. From her mother, she learned the skills of preserving garden produce: the canning, drying, pickling and brining processes of the time. She also learned to cook and to care for the younger children.

These skills from the nineteenth century, gained by both Rosie and her future husband Paul in their childhood, were extremely important to their survival during the setbacks caused by the Great Depression and the 1937 Kentucky Flood.

Making whiskey had been a traditional skill of Edward's ancestors, and the quality of his own whiskey was widely known. When the prohibition of alcoholic drinks was imposed by law, his liquor was in even greater demand. Many musicians who played in the larger cities knew of Edward and his high quality product because they had grown up in Grayson County in the Tar Hill and the Mt. Hebron communities. Edward hired extra help to supply the demand, but both the farm and the still required long hours of his own hard labor.

As a young teenager Rosie took on responsibilities far beyond her age. When her younger brother, Joe Ed, while riding astride a log that was being sawed for firewood, slipped his fingers under the crosscut saw, three fingers were severed around the first joint. Rosie acted as the doctor, reattaching the fingers, which healed successfully. The only obvious after-effect was that a couple of the fingers grew two fingernails each.

Another instance of Rosas medical skills involved Bernard Portman, who was born and raised on the farm adjacent to the Milliner farm. Bernard, as a young boy, had fallen into the pigpen with a cantankerous sow that had a litter of new pigs. The sow attacked Bernard, biting one of his ears and tearing it nearly off. Bernard's father, having heard of Rosie's success with Joe Ed's fingers, asked her to re-attach Bernard's ear. She burned the needle in flames and soaked the thread in moonshine whiskey to sterilize it, then re-attached the ear. Bernard, when he was nearly 75 years old, showed others the scar on that ear, then barely visible.

In the late 1940s, Rosie's medical abilities came into play when Norbert, her son, jumped from an apple tree onto a pile of scrap lumber. In one of the boards, a long, rusty ten-penny nail was exposed. The nail penetrated Norbert's foot and extended more than an inch through the top of the foot behind the middle toe.

Rosie approached the problem cautiously. There was no transportation to a doctor and probably no money to pay for formal medical attention. Her solution was to lay Norbert on his back on the ground. With her foot on his crotch, she grasped both ends of the board. She warned, "This will probably hurt more coming out than it did going in!" In an instant, she jerked the nail out. The horizon dimmed and the daylight faded into darkness for a few seconds as Norbert experienced the intense pain.

Rosie explained to Norbert that the wound would need to remain open, both top and bottom, so that the puss and the rust from the nail could drain out. The wound would slowly heal from the inside out.

Then Rosie went to the smokehouse where she shaved two thin slivers from the salt-pork. These slivers were positioned over the wound, top and bottom, and secured with strips of cloth torn from a worn out shirt. The wound was redressed every day for a couple of weeks until the drainage showed no rust particles. Norbert hobbled on his sore foot until the wound healed.

Marriage

Rosie married Paul Clark in 1932 when she was 18 years old. The wedding dinner, like all the local wedding dinners of the time, was held at the bride's home. Her parents gave them a heifer to raise as a milk cow, and they moved into the abandoned log cabin where her parents had lived after they were married. They carried water from the same spring and tended the same garden spot that Edward and Mary Alta had tended 18 years before.

Rosie lost two babies at childbirth during the next four years. In 1936, a healthy boy, Norbert, was born, and that fall the family moved to Louisville. She described to her children the painful experience of living there in the shadow of the Depression. Daily, hungry men knocked at the door asking to mend the fence or shovel the snow or repair a broken window for the meager pay of a sandwich. In order to help the men maintain their pride and self-respect, Rosie would have them sweep the walk or do other simple tasks while she prepared sandwiches of leftovers from breakfast.

Then, in the spring of 1937, the Ohio River flooded and the industries, most of which were located along the river, were destroyed. Rosie and Paul, after experiencing the consecutive catastrophes of the Depression and a flood, decided to rely on survival skills learned from their ancestors. They returned to the land where they had grown up, scratching a living from the thin, hilly, rocky farms of northeastern Grayson County, Kentucky, between Meeting and Clifty Creeks.

During her 20 years of marriage, whether living in the long abandoned log cabin or living in the modern house of a landlord, Rosie maintained her pride, her self confidence and the respect of the community. She kept friendships with former school mates and gained new friendships with every move. Her jolly, friendly personality provided the invitation for relaxed, open conversations. Her friends included backwoods, under-educated relatives and neighbors, as well the landlords and teachers in the community. Her extroverted personality supported her optimistic attitude towards the difficulties of her life: two still births, the Depression, the flood and World War II.

I HEARD MY MOMMA SAY.....

Well I heard my Momma say

Yea, I heard my Momma say

"We gonna rise and shine,

Gonna toe the line"

Yea, I heard my Momma say

Well I heard my Momma say

Yea, I heard my Momma say

"We gonna go to school

Learn the golden rule"

Yea, I heard my Momma say

Well, I heard my Momma say

Yea, I heard my Momma say

"We gonna toe the line

Save a shiny dime"

Yea, I heard my Momma say

Well I heard my Momma say

Yea I heard my Momma say

"We gonna sing and play

Till the break of day"

Yea, I heard my Momma say

Well, I heard my Momma say
Yea, I heard my Momma say
"We gonna plant the corn
In the early morn"
Yea, I heard my Momma say.

--Song by Norbert Clark

2
PAUL

The Young Farmer

Paul was the seventh child born to Ike and Janie Clark, arriving as Ike was nearing the end of his career as a professional traveling carpenter who built church steeples, wooden railroad bridges, depots, houses and barns.

Growing up, Paul learned many skills from Ike, but by the time Paul was old enough to remember, his father was already sometimes restricted to a wheelchair. His hard work had taken its toll on his health and his joints were racked with the pain caused by rheumatism. Anticipating the time when he could no longer work, Ike planted a large orchard on his small farm as an additional source of income. Paul remembered Ike sitting in his wheelchair as he grafted buds and sprouts on the fruit trees to balance the symmetry and improve the productivity.

When Paul was about twelve years old and in the sixth grade, he was taken out of school to help support the family. The Clark home had burned at this time, destroying all their clothes and household possessions. The family escaped in their night clothes. It is unclear whether the fire contributed to his parent's decision to remove Paul from school, but his older brothers and sisters had married and left the community, so Paul had to become responsible for the farm work.

One of Paul's chores was to take the corn to the mill at Hardin Springs where the corn was ground into meal to make bread for the family. One bushel of white corn in a long cotton bag was divided in the middle and hung over the back of the mule. Paul sat on the center of the bag. The miller kept one-fourth of the meal as payment for the grinding. Corn was an important part of the daily diet of the Clark family: cornbread, corn fritters, corn mush, hominy, hominy grits and parched corn were common dishes and snacks.

Hickory Cane corn was the preferred variety of white corn. While other varieties were planted for livestock feed, a patch of Hickory Cane corn was always planted for eating by the family. When it was cooked dry in a greased and salted pan on high heat, the dry corn turned into a brittle, crunchy snack food. When popcorn wasn't available, parched corn was a common snack for Paul and his teenage friends.

A Musical Family

Paul grew up in a musical family that owned and played an organ along with stringed instruments. Their Victrola had many records. Paul learned to play the fiddle at a young age, after his older brother, Bernard, had traded a quart of moonshine whiskey to the local preacher for an old fiddle. While the older members of the family were in the fields working, Paul, with his mother's permission, learned to play the fiddle, and, as a young teenager, he played the fiddle for local square dances.

Third Degree Burns

About this time, Paul suffered an accident that left him with third degree burns over the lower half of his body. For months he laid on pallets on the floor. His teenage sister, Iva, was his primary attendant, applying the medicines and healing lotions over his blistered legs. All the hair follicles on his lower body were destroyed and the solid scar covered half his body.

The cause for the burns was remembered differently by different relatives. Some explained that Paul was burned when a tub of hot wash water was spilled on him. Others said that Paul, when helping around the moonshine still, was burned when a barrel of hot mash spilled on him.

Maturity and Responsibility

Forty years later when Norbert, his son, was working in a grocery store in Clarkson, Kentucky a Mr. Royalty approached him. "So, your name is Clark. You're from over on the ridge? Did you know Paul Clark?"

Norbert's response was "Yes, he was my father."

Mr. Royalty explained that he was a little older than Paul, and that he had lived in the community, growing up near the Clark family. He described Paul as "the most mature, the most responsible" teenager in the community. During many visits to the store during almost two years, Mr. Royalty's message of admiration for Paul was always the same.

That maturity and sense of responsibility was Paul's trademark. He registered and voted in the 1932 election when he was only twenty years old. He was strongly opposed to the "hands off" policies of President Herbert Hoover and, although his family was strongly Republican, Paul voted for Roosevelt, a Democrat.

"Right is right" was his philosophy. In his quiet, friendly way, he advised a middle aged bachelor neighbor who had contacted tuberculosis and had decided that death was his only option, that modern medical technology could cure the disease and provide many healthy years. The neighbor responded and lived many years.

Paul advised an illiterate neighbor who had a large family and a small income that he should file an income tax form. By filing and paying a small social security assessment, he would be eligible for a social security payment when he was no longer able to work on the farm. The neighbor did that and expressed his appreciation in later years.

Paul assured his sister, whose husband had been killed, that he and the community were prepared to help her and her family of five children. She must not give up and lose community respect. Self-confidence and self-respect were her only means to a stable and predictable future. She responded, and later entered a second, more stable marriage.

He also advised Rosie's two bachelor brothers that their habits of binge drinking were putting them at extremely high risk. They ignored the advice. Both were dead in a few years, the result of their drinking behavior.

When the game warden asked about the number of squirrels and squirrel hunters in the woods, Paul said: "If the squirrels are too thick around my corn field, I will kill a few of them, no matter what the season. I raised them, since they eat my corn, my walnuts, my hickory nuts—and I will eat a few of them when the time is right."

After Rosie died, Paul, contrary to the advice of many relatives and friends, kept the family together. He accepted the full responsibility and adjusted his life to fulfill the obligations.

Geography and "Haints"

The community of Mount Hebron where Paul grew up was located on the old mission trail dating back to the late seventeen hundreds. Both Protestant and Catholic missionaries traveled the trail which had previously been an Indian trail.

Mount Hebron was also an extremely hilly region at the confluence of three major streams: the Rough River, Clifty Creek and Meeting Creek. Millions of years of erosion had cut deep 'hollers' surrounded by tall sandstone cliffs. Strong evidence of Stone Age Indians in residence under and around the cliffs was obvious when Paul was growing up. Neighbors, ignoring all interests of archeology and history, dug under the cliffs exposing campsites and graves. Their only interests were a few beads, arrowheads or stone tools.

An old Protestant cemetery at the top of the hill near the Clark farm contained a large pile of sandstone rocks. Folklore in the community described this as the grave of a child of the first settlers who passed through the area in the late seventeen hundreds.

The mystery of the region was enhanced not only by the remoteness and the strong archeological presence of the Indians, but also by the presence of plumes of highly colorful phosphorescent gas that erupted from certain sinkholes under certain weather conditions. To the mostly uneducated population, this introduced an element of superstition and supernatural activity that influenced their daily actions. Many people would not pass the area after dark. Even Paul and his family, who were not superstitious, were sometimes in doubt about what was happening.

Any opportunity to play a trick on a friend or a neighbor was never missed. For example, Paul's older brother, Bernard, had once ridden his mule to a country square dance across Clifty Creek. During the evening a loud thunder storm resulted in a heavy rain. Their mother Janie became worried that Bernard, who was late returning home, had experienced trouble crossing the swollen creek. She woke Paul and sent him to investigate.

When Paul reached the top of the hill near the cemetery and the sinkholes where the phosphorescent gas periodically erupted, he heard a mule or a horse in the distance. He decided to wait at the top of the hill until the rider approached. Since many people traveled the road, the rider might not be Bernard.

The evening was cool and Paul pulled his overall jacket around his head and waited in the middle of the road at the top of the hill in the dark. About the time the rider came within speaking distance, the dark, fast moving clouds opened, exposing a full moon and visibility that compared to full daylight.

The rider yelled "Whoa!" and stopped his horse abruptly. Paul recognized Bernard's voice and proceeded to pull his coat from his head changing from a headless ghost to a human form. Bernard shouted, "Is that you, Paul? I was ready to turn and gallop in the opposite direction!" Mysterious apparitions like this were usually explainable, but they also opened topics of conversation and presented ideas for those tricksters who cared to repeat the suspense.

Another story was told by a neighbor who was riding his horse through the area one dark night. A person whom he thought he recognized as a neighbor was standing beside the road. The horseman asked the neighbor if he wanted a ride. Without speaking, the man mounted the horse behind the saddle. Two miles down the road the man behind the saddle had not yet responded to questions nor entered into conversations with the horseman. At an unexpected location, the questionable form slipped off the rear of the horse and disappeared into the darkness, never speaking nor acknowledging the horseman.

Stories like this were told for entertainment. The absence of radio or television or other forms of canned entertainment provided opportunities for the creativity of homegrown storytellers.

Once Paul himself, returning on a rainy night from a friend's house, decided to climb through the fence from the muddy road into a pasture field. He was again passing the area of greatest superstition. In the cloudy night, a white form appeared in the darkness in front of him. Paul approached slowly and cautiously, stopping to study the white form. He suspected that someone who knew where he had been, had decided to scare him.

"O.K.", he said. "I give up. Who is it?" The form stood motionless. Paul, remembering that he had kicked a rock a couple of steps behind him, stepped backward until he felt the rock with his foot. He picked up the rock. "O.K., you're going to get this rock if you don't speak up!" The form stood motionless. Paul threw the rock hitting the white, motionless form. A white mule, suddenly awakened from sleep, galloped across the field. The mysterious form was more natural than supernatural.

Marriage to Rosie

In the fall before Paul and Rosie were married, Paul went to Richmond, Indiana to earn money working on the farms so he could buy a suit for his wedding. On the morning of the wedding, Paul wore his new suit with his last ten dollar bill stuffed in the pocket.

It was customary to give the pastor a couple of dollars as a token of appreciation for performing the wedding. Paul gave the pastor the ten dollar bill, expecting change. The pastor, without looking, stuffed the money into his pocket and Paul went home penniless on his wedding day.

Paul's parents gave them a dozen laying hens and a rooster. With the heifer as a gift from Rosie's parents, they set up housekeeping in the log cabin where Rosie's parents had lived.

Familiar Land

Paul's mother, Janie Langley, grew up on a farm near St. Paul Church. She remembered carrying water from a fresh water spring to the workmen who helped her father build a dog-trot cabin (a cabin built in two parts connected by a breezeway between the two) in 1880. After sharecropping for 14 years, Paul bought this old Langley farm in 1946.

Janie, while living with Paul's family in her childhood home, led her grandchildren through the woods pointing out the maple trees her family had tapped. She followed the trails that her family had travelled with the oxen pulling a sled with wooden barrels to collect the maple sap. She hesitated under the cliffs where her family had boiled the sap into maple syrup.

Janie also pointed out the holes in Meeting Creek where Paul's children were likely to catch fish. She relived the history of the old farm and the history of her childhood.

DADDY PLAYED THE FIDDLE

My Daddy played the fiddle, Lawd,

How he'd make it ring.

It made me want to dance a jig;

It made me want to sing.

I know he'll play the fiddle there,

I know he'll make it ring,

See saints in Heaven dance a jig,

And hear the Angels sing!

Paul met St. Peter at the gate;

Pete's face was straight and stern.

"Now Paul, you lay that fiddle down;

In hell those fiddles burn!"

You'll find our saints are straightly laced;

You'll find they kneel and pray.

Just lay that fiddle by the gate;

The junk man comes today!"

Paul refused St. Peter's plea

To lay his fiddle down.

He played a tune called "Soldier's Joy"

While dancing round and round

The saints in heaven jumped for joy,

"Please play that tune again."

They clapped their hands, they danced around

'Cause music is no sin.

They begged St. Peter, "Let him in;

He's such a happy lad.

We need his music in the clouds

So folks forget we're dead."

That's why there's music way up there

To which we all aspire.

That's why we hear the angels sing

In heaven's angel choir.

-Song by Norbert Clark

3

UNCLE JOHN'S HILL FARM

In the spring of 1937, after the big flood destroyed much of the industry beside the Ohio River in Louisville, Paul and Rosie moved from Louisville back to Grayson County. Paul had worked in a factory located near the river in Portland, a residential and manufacturing section of the city in its northwest corner. Pictures of the '37 flood taken on Main and Market Streets, several blocks from the river, showed that the flood waters reached the second story windows. The residents could step out of those high windows into the boats.

That flood and the poor labor conditions resulting from the depression led Paul and Rosie to return to their birthplace in Grayson County. Both had grown up working on hill farms, learning the skills their ancestors found necessary for survival.

With their nine-month-old son Norbert and carrying a few handbags, they boarded the L&N (Louisville and Nashville) train to Elizabethtown. As they rode the train south along the Ohio River in the bottomland near Kosmosdale, at the confluence of the Ohio and the Salt Rivers, they described the flood as "Lapping at the cross-ties, giving you the feeling that you were in a boat on the ocean." They rode one of the last trains south to run on those tracks until after the flood. At Elizabethtown, they transferred to the E-Town-Paducah line to Big Clifty.

For a few weeks after their return to the farming community, they lived with Iva, Paul's sister, and her husband Carl Hazelwood. Carl and Ivy had also returned to the country because of the flood.

Arrangements were soon made to rent a farm from Paul's Uncle, John Langley. He and his wife, Dora, were becoming too old to work their large hill farm in Hardin County. They had no sons to manage the farm and their only daughter, May, lived and worked in the city.

So Paul and Rosie with their son, Norbert, moved into a small two-room house that had been abandoned when John and Dora built a larger, more modern house. The old house was located a few hundred yards north of the main farmhouse on a steep hill facing west. It was near a fresh-water spring where they would get their water. The steep hillside field around the house had once been cleared and cultivated. Because of its rocks, this field had been abandoned, allowing the sassafras, the hickory, the persimmon bushes and the blackberry briars to reclaim the land.

A narrow dirt wagon path led from the main dirt road up the hill to the house. The house itself was being used to store tobacco and corn fodder. The wooden tobacco sticks and the scraps of corn fodder had to be removed from the house prior to moving in.

Rosie and Paul covered the inside of the walls with heavy construction paper to keep out the wind and the wildlife. A small iron step-stove for cooking and heating was installed by extending a stovepipe through the wall. The brick flue would be repaired before the next winter. They lived in this small house, farming with Uncle John, using his horses and equipment until John decided to sell the farm in the fall of 1938.

Traveling Across Meeting-Creek to Church

From their farm on the north side of Meeting Creek, Rosie and Paul traveled about two miles south to attend Mass at St. Paul Church in Grayson County. Several other families from the area also attended the church, riding in their farm wagons, pulled by their workhorses.

The county road progressed slowly down the hill eastward from Uncle John's house to a shallow point at Tood's Ford, where it was possible to cross Meeting-Creek. Many other roads on both sides of the creek all converged near that ford.

The roads themselves were a problem. Periodically, the farmers scheduled a few workdays to maintain them by digging drainage ditches to drain the mud holes and then filling the holes with fieldstones. The workers broke down the rock ledges where erosion and daily traffic had caused the ledges to become too steep for the farm wagons. These roads were on private property and followed the path of least resistance up and down the hills. Most roads crossed the streams at the shallow fords, eliminating the need for bridges. These roads were considered public roads even though they made their way through private property.

Several large Catholic families (the Cripps, Harris, Burkhead and Drury families) also crossed Tood's Ford on their journey to St. Paul Church. For walkers, a swinging bridge located about a half-mile to the east provided a shorter footpath to the Church.

After crossing Meeting-Creek at Tood's Ford, the steep, rocky, crooked road progressed slowly uphill. It passed the fresh water spring from which young Janie Langley, Paul's mother, had carried

21

water to the workmen who were building her father Charles Langley's log house and barn in 1880. At the top of the hill the road passed between that old log house and the log barn.

After passing the Langley homestead, the crooked dirt road passed the houses and small farms of Asa Clark, John Cub Clark and William Andy Pearl. It joined the St. Paul Road at the home of Isadore Clark. The distance from Uncle John's house to the Church was approximately four miles on the hilly road. The footpath across the fields was half that distance.

Since the route across the swinging bridge to Church increased the distance from Uncle John's house, Paul felled a tree across the creek near the house. This provided a foot-log for crossing the creek when the water at Tood's ford was too deep for the farm wagon.

On one Sunday after a heavy winter rain, Rosie and Paul with young Norbert were crossing the swollen creek, walking the foot-log on their way to Church. Paul, carrying Norbert, slipped from the frosty and slippery foot-log into the swollen creek. He was able to cling to the log, holding his son above the rushing water, until Rosie could rescue Norbert and Paul could escape the swollen creek. On their way home in cold wet clothes, they stopped in Uncle John and Aunt Dora's living room to warm up beside the stove.

A Young Son's Memories

Norbert remembered two events that happened in that fall before they moved from Uncle John's farm. These memories were like flashes—one episode, with five-second pictures in his memory. He was then almost two and a half years old.

The first memory: on a warm fall afternoon Paul had been picking corn and scooping it into the crib and Rosie was milking the cow outside the barn. Some of the corn nubbins were pitched on the ground to pacify the cow while she was milked. Then the cow, while still eating, scattered one of the nubbins a distance from the pile.

Norbert's sudden impulse was to pick the nubbin from the ground and give it to the cow. The cow swung her head at flies, accidently hanging her horn in the corner of Norbert's mouth, knocking him to the ground. The wound healed rapidly without stitches, but left a minor permanent scar.

The second memory happened a few days later when the fall apples were ripening. Rosie, Paul and Norbert walked in the evening after supper to visit Uncle John and Aunt Dora who were sitting on their front porch in their rocking chairs. As usual, Norbert was the focus of their warm smiles and attention, a substitute for the grandchildren they never had.

After their loving greetings on the front porch, Rosie and Aunt Dora took Norbert through the house to the orchard in the backyard to pick up apples from the ground. Collecting and eating the ripe apples was a favorite and memorable moment for Norbert.

During the year that they lived on Uncle John's farm, Paul and Rosie reestablished themselves as subsistence farmers. They earned a share of the farm crops to feed their chickens and the milk cow. They raised a garden in order to can, dry, preserve, pickle and store enough food for winter. Six years after their marriage, this year was a reenactment of the first year of their marriage in 1932.

MOUNTAIN HOME

High up yonder on the mountain,
High up yonder on the hill,
High up yonder on the mountain
Stands a cabin on the hill.

High up yonder where the sun is slowly rising,
High up yonder stands a cabin on the hill.
High up yonder where the settlers raised their children
Now the cabin stands; the front porch swing is still.

High up yonder where the mountain flowers are blooming
High up yonder stands a cabin on the hill
High up yonder where the redbuds paint the hillside,
Where the birds sing of the beauty of these hills.

High up yonder where the mountain streams are flowing,
High up yonder stands a cabin on the hill,
High up yonder where the owls call in the evening,
Where you wake-up to the songs of the whippoorwills.

High up yonder on the hillside in the mountains,

High up yonder stands a cabin on the hill.

High up yonder stands a monument to history,

To the history of the settlers in these hills.

-- Song by Norbert Clark

4
THE BILL WHITFILL FARM

Moving Day

That fall, the Clark family moved to a smaller and rougher hill farm in Grayson County near Clifty Creek by the community of Mount Hebron. The farm wagon, pulled by Uncle John's horses, was used for the move. All the household items were loaded on the wagon, kept from falling out by use of the sideboards that were also used for gathering corn.

The iron bedstead, the kitchen utensils, the small step-cooking stove, the homemade table and the straight-backed chairs with white oak splints, the feather bed and the straw mattress were piled high. Paul's fiddle, for which he had no case, was carefully wrapped and placed between the rungs of the upturned chairs. Paul, Rosie and Norbert sat on the seat board pushed to the extreme front position.

Under the seat, a chicken coop contained about a dozen Dominique hens and a rooster. They squawked in fear and excitement at the strange experience. The milk cow with a rope halter was tied to the rear of the wagon by a rope short enough to prevent entanglement. The farm dog, Spot, followed the caravan reluctantly at first, but soon followed willingly. A couple of bags of corn were included to feed the milk cow, the horses and the chickens.

The first leg of the trip was downhill to the east across Meeting Creek at Tood's Ford. After crossing the creek the road turned west on a level farm road around the edge of the bottomland. They passed the stumps of the maple trees where young Janie Langley, Paul's mother, had driven the oxen collecting the maple sap in the late eighteen hundreds. They passed sandstone cliffs under which Janie's family had boiled the sap into syrup.

Upon leaving the creek bottoms, the horses were confronted with the steepest hill of the trip. The steep, rough road went straight up the hill, climbing rock ledges and maneuvering through ditches. It was a challenge for a team even when pulling an empty wagon.

To prepare for the climb, the family climbed down from the wagon. Paul would drive the horses while walking uphill on the ground. The milk cow didn't adjust to the plan, instead continuously pulling backward. So she was untied and led by hand up the hill.

The horses were extended to the limits of their strength. They could progress only a few feet with each pull. Paul, driving and operating the brake from the ground, encouraged the horses through each pull and rested them often. When they had regained their breath, the effort was repeated. After several pulls—with the rocks dislodging under the horses' hooves and the horses falling to their knees—the steep rough hill was climbed.

The remainder of the trip over mostly level, well maintained county roads progressed with less excitement until the last half mile. After passing the old Pool's Mill site at Clifty Creek, they turned right around the lower edge of a north hillside. The seldom traveled road followed the edge of the woods and the trees beside the road had grown to the extent that low hanging branches needed to be cut with the ax to allow the high-piled wagon to pass.

On one occasion, the overhead branches were growing from the trunk of the tree too high to be cut with the ax. The wagon, with its tall load, was allowed to push slowly past the bending branches, but then the tension in one bending branch released in a slingshot motion. The rapidly sweeping branch picked up the cotton mill bag which contained Paul's fiddle. The fiddle was flung to the rocky hillside, breaking the neck of the instrument.

Following this excitement, the horses proceeded slowly around the north hillside. They crossed the spring branch and approached the long abandoned log cabin. It was here where Paul and Rosie's second son, Samuel, was born a year later in November.

Another Abandoned Cabin

A middle aged bachelor named Joe Esker Conder owned this farm. He had bought it from Bill Whitfill when Bill moved to a more productive farm a couple of miles east on Salt River Road.

Like the Langley house from which they had moved, this old one-room log cabin had been abandoned for several years. Most recently, it had been used for storing tobacco and corn fodder. Prior to moving, Paul and Joe Esker had cleared the cabin of debris and replaced the broken glass. Because the thumb latch on the front door was broken, a wooden button was substituted inside. This meant that when a family member went outside, the button had to be turned by someone on the inside to allow reentry. Paul and Rosie soon attached a chain on the outside until the latch was repaired.

The same kind of heavy construction paper that Paul and Rosie had used to cover the inside of the Langley house was used to cover the inside of the Whitfill cabin. Their small iron cook stove was installed in a side-room kitchen barely large enough to also hold a table and chairs.

A flue collar for a stovepipe had been installed in the original fieldstone chimney in the main part of the cabin and a sheet iron stove was installed there for heating. The iron bedstead where everyone slept sat in the corner of the log cabin. The straight chairs with bottoms of hickory splints were moved from the kitchen to the living room when needed. When they were filled, guests sat on the bed.

A narrow shelf-type table was nailed to the kitchen wall opposite the cook stove. This was where the galvanized water bucket sat with a gray granite dipper. The shelf was used both for the wash pan for washing hands and for the dishpan for washing dishes.

A small window above the table looked south, up a steep hillside overgrown with dry broom sage grass, blackberry briars and many varieties of bushes. The hillside had originally been cultivated but now had not been planted for several years. A fresh water spring, from which the drinking water was carried, flowed from the hillside and trickled across the road east of the log cabin.

Paul built and installed a V-shaped wooden trough under the eve of the side-room to direct rainwater into a wooden barrel. Pans of the rainwater were heated on the cook stove for Saturday night baths in a number two washtub. Homemade lye soap, a byproduct of the winter hog slaughter, was used for washing everything. The extra pork fat was boiled with caustic soda until it congealed. When it cooled, the soap was cut into bars.

Moving to this home took several additional trips after the first load of furniture and household items, the milk cow, the dog and the chickens. A few loads of corn and fodder were hauled by a different road bypassing the steep, eroded Harris Hill. This road, mainly a farm road, progressed west on the north side of Meeting Creek for almost a mile through the Langley and the Drake bottom land. It crossed Meeting Creek at the Smallwood Ford and climbed the longer, flatter Burkhead hill to the level upland road. This route was longer but much easier for the horses.

After the move was completed, Uncle John's horses and wagon were returned and Paul and Rosie prepared for the winter. In the absence of a cellar, the garden produce moved from the Langley farm—the onions and potatoes, the turnips and parsnips, the squash and sweet potatoes—were stored in the attic above the heated cabin. The canned fruits and vegetables, pickles, relishes, jams and jellies were stored on shelves in the kitchen. The crocks of kraut and pickles with a few black iron pots and skillets were stored on the floor under the washstand. A cloth apron that draped to the floor was tacked around the edges of the washstand.

Adventures in the Barn

The small barn on the Whitfill farm was a more modern structure that had replaced the original log barn. It had four stalls on each side of a driveway wide enough for a wide wagon load of corn fodder or tobacco to be hauled in. One stall had been converted to a corn crib by installing a wooden floor. Six stalls were opened to the driveway, having walls only about four feet high so that the horses could extend their heads into the driveway. A seventh stall was totally enclosed from the ground up to the loft. Its door had been tightly closed with three cross-boards that had been fastened with large nails.

That closed stall had housed the Whitfill family's milk cow, which had been bitten by a rabid fox. She had been quarantined and the Whitfills were waiting for two weeks to see if the cow would develop rabies, while hoping that she would survive the bite. Then the cow's behavior changed from being a gentle milk cow to the actions of a raging bull that attacked everything that moved. The blind rage and the foaming mouth were clear symptoms of rabies. For fear that another animal might contact rabies, this stall was later only used for storing small farm tools and wooden tobacco sticks.

A small chicken house that was also used as an outhouse sat closer to the log cabin between the house and the barn. In the front of the chicken house close to the cabin was a pile of long tree trunks. They had been dragged from the woods, unseasoned, for a supply of winter wood for heating and cooking. Later, Herbert and Joe Ed, Rosie's younger brothers, sawed some of the logs into firewood. At other times, Rosie, the oldest of Edward and Mary Alta's nine children and experienced in the use of the crosscut saw, pulled the two-man saw opposite Paul.

Profits from the Farm

Cream, skimmed from the milk, was an important source of farm income. To increase the quantity of the cream and improve the butterfat content, the crushed corn fed to the milk cow was supplemented with high-protein soybean meal bought at Charlie Drake's store and mill. The hens were also fed a supplement of high-protein laying mash with their corn to increase their egg production. Paul and Rosie sold the extra eggs from the hens to the store, using the money to buy the extra feed for the animals, and flour, salt and sugar for the family.

The eggs and the cream, with the occasional opossum skin caught with the help of the family dog, provided money to purchase necessities. Shotgun shells counted as essentials, since they provided the occasional rabbit or squirrel for a pot of game and dumplings.

A few steel traps, a box trap and a few snares were set to catch a rabbit or a quail. The traps were baited with an apple or ear of corn.

These survival tactics, used by Rosie and Paul during the winter of 1938-39, were the same as those used by their ancestors many years before. The old log cabin added to the authenticity of that pioneer setting.

Christmas Dinner

Rosie's parents sent a fat goose for her family's Christmas dinner. In addition to the roast goose, Rosie prepared her dish featured at all holiday dinners: the Irish potato salad. The potatoes were mashed and flavored with bacon drippings and mustard. They were molded into a turtle-shape on a large platter and circular slices of boiled eggs were arranged in decorative circles around the potatoes. Brown crumbs of crisp bacon were sprinkled over the potatoes. The adults would sometimes delay their eating of the pretty dish out of appreciation for its beauty. The beauty of the dish made it more desirable to the children.

Rosie did not own a cookbook. She reproduced the old recipes using skills learned from her mother and grandmother.

COUNTRY MEANS...

Born to live this country life.

Born to carry this heavy load.

Born to live among these hills.

Born to walk this country road.

Country means a rooster crows;

The sun will surely rise.

Country means the mountain fog

Lifts slowly to the skies.

Country means a whippoorwill,

A bullfrog by the lake.

Country means a turtle dove

Cooing for its mate.

Country means an old log house.

The children in warm beds.

Country means a warm fireplace

Hot logs a glowing red.

Country means a garden plot;

Country means a barn

Country means a gentle mule

To till this hillside farm

Country means you walk dirt roads;

The stars are bright at night.

Country means your teenage friends

Yearn for those city lights.

Country means a lonesome song;

Country means romance

Country means a fiddle tune;

Hold hands and let's square dance.

-Song by Norbert Clark

5
DIGGING IN\

The Classic Landlord

After the move was completed and Uncle John's horses and wagon were returned, Paul used the horses owned by Joe Esker Conder, the landlord. Joe Esker owned a large, gray Percheron broodmare that foaled a colt most every year. If an extra horse was not needed on the farm, the colt was sold as a yearling. Joe Esker always had a good team of workhorses in addition to one or two young horses in training.

Joe Esker's prize possession was a team of buggy horses and a two-seated, covered surrey. The horses were a perfectly matched team of sorrels with white stockings and broad blazed faces. This team and surrey was used primarily to go to church or as fast transportation to the courthouse, where Joe Esker was active and influential in politics. On Sundays, Paul and Rosie walked out of the hills from the cabin to Joe Esker's house and joined him for the ride to the church in the surrey behind the classy team.

Joe Esker soon became aware of the honesty, integrity, and the energy and ambitions of Paul and Rosie. He treated them as family rather than as tenants. They eventually moved from the crude cabin into his farm house. He joined them for all meals and family activities. They became the family that Joe Esker, as a bachelor, did not have.

35

During the winter Paul had access to Joe Esker's workhorses and a wagon or sled as needed. The typical procedure was to borrow a team hitched to the sled to haul the bags of corn, the bucket of cream or the case of eggs from the cabin over the rough roads to Joe Esker's barn. The produce was then transferred to the appropriate wagon or buggy depending on the load.

Burning Plant Beds

Late in the winter, before plowing the fields and preparing them for planting the corn, the bushes and briars that had grown in the abandoned fields for a few years were cut and stacked in an unused field. Trees in the woods around the edge of the fields or in the fencerows were trimmed and that brush was added to the pile. The tree trunks and poles themselves were hauled or dragged to the house for firewood. When the pile of brush grew to the height of the fence posts and covered an area as large as the driveway of the barn, it was burned, making a plant bed for tobacco and garden plants.

The burning was intended to kill all grass and weed roots and seeds so tobacco and garden plants could grow unimpaired. Most of the area was planted with tobacco seeds, so small that a teaspoon of seeds would cover the entire seedbed. The tiny seeds were mixed with dry soil from the plant bed to ensure even distribution.

A small area around the edge of the tobacco plant bed was planted with garden seeds ordered from the seed catalogue: lettuce, cabbage and radishes. Other seeds like pepper, corn, beans and tomato seeds were saved from the previous year's crop.

The tobacco plant bed was encircled with poles about six inches in diameter. A canvas cover about nine feet wide was nailed to the poles. This canvas provided protection from unexpected late frosts and increased the temperatures of the soil for faster germination and growth. Planted in early March, the tobacco plants would be ready to set out in a field in the middle of May.

The garden plants matured earlier, so the cabbage, tomato and pepper plants were transplanted in the garden by the first of May. The radishes, lettuce and cabbages that had been planted around the edge of the tobacco bed were mature enough to eat by early May as well.

Potatoes—the Staple

Potatoes were a staple for the subsistence farmers, included in at least one meal every day. Fried potatoes with scrambled eggs or potato pancakes with sorghum molasses were two favorite breakfast meals. They were planted in the warm sandy soil on a dry south hillside as early as the first of March. Small new potatoes were dug from the roots of the potato plant by early June, without harming the plant. A late crop of potatoes was planted in early July for harvest in the fall. These potatoes grown in the dry summer and fall seasons were more stable in winter storage than the early potatoes.

Rosie and Paul stored the potatoes in the attic above the heated cabin under a few bundles of corn fodder. When an attic or a cellar was not available, the potatoes were stored underground.

Tenant Farmers

Toward the end of the first winter in their cabin, Paul and Rosie started preparing for the spring planting season. When Joe Esker's horses were busy in the spring, they depended heavily on the generosity of Rosie's family. Her father had an extra team of horses and two teenage sons, Herbert and Joe Ed, who were old enough to handle the teams and operate all of the manual farm equipment.

The boys would arrive at the field early in the morning, helping Paul dig bushes and briars in preparation for plowing the long abandoned and hilly fields. After clearing the brush, the field was plowed and prepared for planting with a harrow and a drag. The corn was planted with a single shovel plow followed by a one-row drill that dropped in the seeds.

At lunch time, the horses were watered, fed and rested and Rosie delivered a lunch to the workers in the field. The lunch always included a large pan of cornbread and a jar of milk. The rest of the lunch usually consisted of a pot of black-eyed peas or navy beans that had been harvested the previous fall. The dry beans or peas had hung from the ceiling in the kitchen in a paper flour sack to protect them from the field mice that had easy access to the log cabin. The meal was accompanied by a blackberry or peach cobbler using canned fruit harvested the previous summer at the Langley farm.

The rear end-gate was removed from the wagon bed when the meal was served. The workers could either stand around the wagon to eat or find a level place on the ground to set their bowls and glasses of milk.

After a fast lunch for the workers and an additional drink of water for the horses, the work continued. Sometimes the broodmare with a suckling colt was part of one of the teams. The colt ran free beside the mare and its energetic antics provided entertainment for the hardworking men.

About three weeks after the corn had been planted, Herbert and Joe Ed returned to cultivate the crop. They drove a team hitched to a wagon hauling a single-shovel plow and a one-row harrow. The team was Bob, a mule, and Dolly, the broodmare with her colt.

Norbert, now almost three years old, was allowed to go to the cornfield in the wagon with them. The single-shovel plow was used to "bust the middles" and the one-row harrow followed to level the upturned earth. The intention was to uproot the growth of grass and weeds in the middles between the corn rows.

The small corn plants were at risk of being covered if more dirt was moved with larger plows. The next cultivation when the plants were one foot tall would involve plowing closely on both sides of the plants with a double shovel plow. This methodical process, done row after row, would cover the grass and weeds that grew in the corn rows.

While Norbert remained in the wagon the colt was sometimes allowed to run free. Periodically, it would become excited, running rambunctiously across the cornfield and destroying many corn plants. So Herbert tied a rope between the colt's halter and the wagon wheel to keep it nearby. The colt soon made friends with Norbert, nuzzling him gently and allowing Norbert to pet him.

When Rosie delivered lunch to the boys at noon, Norbert went home with her for the afternoon. While Rosie washed the dishes after lunch, Norbert pulled a chair alongside the wash shelf. Standing in the chair beside her, looking out the window, up the hill towards the workers, he told his mother about his morning adventure in the cornfield: "And Uncle Herbert hitched old Bob to the plow and started plowing down the row. Uncle Joe Ed hitched Dolly to the harrow and followed Uncle Herbert. The colt ran around the horses kicking his feet high and stepping on the corn."

The enthusiastic description would continue until Rosie finished the dishes. That she interrupted or asked questions made no difference. "And the colt made friends with me! His hair was soooo soft! His nose was warrrrm! His eyes were blaaack! He was my friennnnnd!"

The brothers finished cultivating the corn and returned home in the evening not knowing the most important contribution of their labors: a friendship.

New Calf, Chicks, Horses

Spring, with the labor and planning required to start the growing season, was a busy season for Paul. It involved building, burning and seeding the plant beds; clearing, plowing and planting the cornfields; and starting an early garden of potatoes and onions.

Rosie ordered a hundred baby chicks from a mail-order catalogue to sell as frying roosters three months later. The newly hatched chicks could be bought much cheaper as straight roosters. The cost of raising these roosters, fed mostly with cracked corn from the crib and supplemented with a high-protein starter, was minimal.

The sale of the roosters at three or four pounds each about June provided a much needed paycheck. The milk-cow which had a new calf was not producing cream. Many of the hens were in their Spring cycle of reproduction, reducing the egg sales. Selling the frying roosters helped to fill the void in the meager farm income.

The young chicks were delicate. If the temperature dropped, they piled together in the corner of the building for warmth, suffocating in large numbers. If the temperature was too hot, they died prostrate on the floor, gasping for fresh air or oxygen.

Because Rosie bought the chicks early in the spring when the temperature was unpredictable, a heat source was provided. In the middle of the brooder house, Paul installed a kerosene lantern. He hung a galvanized wash tub over the lantern to reflect the heat downward. The chicks huddled under the tub around the warm lantern. The system was monitored day and night at two or three hour intervals until the outside temperature increased.

The roosters were sold at three or four pounds, a tender frying weight. Because they grew at different rates, they were sold in three or four batches. Joe Esker, the landlord, had a standard chicken crate that held about twenty-five roosters.

Joe Esker's horses and wagon were borrowed to transport the roosters to the Drake store at Tar Hill Corners. With the money realized from the sale of the roosters, Paul bought a small pig, just weaned. The pig was housed in one of the empty stalls in the barn and fed corn and table scraps to grow to slaughter weight the next winter.

During the summer it became obvious to Paul that, if he was going to be a farmer, he needed a team of horses. The inconvenience of borrowing from Rosie's parents and adjusting to the schedules of relatives and friends contributed to poor timing and additional work.

Joe Esker helped Paul borrow the money to buy a young team of untrained draft horses. The loan would be repaid when Paul sold the tobacco. During the summer and fall these young horses were trained by hitching them beside the older, trained horses. By winter time, they were trained to the extent that they could be hitched as a team to most farm equipment.

Paul retrieved a riding saddle from the barn of his parents, Ike and Janie. He rode the larger and more gentle gelding, Dock. This provided the convenience of crossing the creeks at the fords of both Clifty and Meeting Creeks. When playing the fiddle for square dances at homes located across the creeks, riding the horse was a major convenience.

HILL COUNTRY SPRING

Oh the grass on the hillsides beginning to stir.

There's work for the family; the cupboard is bare.

We'll all work together; for each other we care

And the maple sap's dripping; there's spring in the air.

Oh, the buds on the maples beginning to swell

The maple sap's dripping, drip, drip in the pail.

Build a fire 'neath the kettle, the steam smells so sweet.

As we stroll through the woodlot, the birds sing twee, tweet.

Oh bring out the farm sled; and harness the mare.

Haul the rocks from the hillside; cut the bush; cut the briar.

Bring out the hill plow and sharpen the share.

And the winter is waning; there's spring in the air.

And the fish on the riffle beginning to spawn

The mushrooms are peeping their heads from the ground.

The wild greens are tender by the creek where it's warm

And springtime is coming; the bees start to swarm.

And the larks in the meadow sing a song to their mate.

The garden is planted; spring rains coming late.

Young calves in the barnyard; mother hens feed young chicks

And the roses are blooming, the lilacs turn pink.

- Song by Norbert Clark

6
USING SURVIVAL SKILLS

Spot, the Protector

The summer was filled with many adventures. When the dog, Spot, barked at something at the north end of the cabin, Rosie sent Norbert to investigate. In the corner by the large fieldstone chimney, the dog was barking at a groundhog that had attempted to dig a new den under the cabin. The groundhog was almost as large as Spot.

When Norbert reported the problem to Rosie, she grabbed the long poker that was once used to place the logs in the fireplace, and rushed outside to help the dog.

As Rosie swung the poker at the groundhog, the dog attacked the animal. It dodged, leaving the dog in the path of the poker. Spot was knocked unconscious and the groundhog ran for the hills unhurt. Rosie, hoping to revive the dog, rushed to the kitchen to get a pail of water to pour on the dog's head. Almost instantly Spot was revived with no noticeable side affects except a knot on his head.

Summer and Fall Routines

Paul spent the summer tending the crops of corn and tobacco on the farm that he had rented. He also worked with Joe Esker on his larger, more productive farm. With the Johnsons, the Langleys and the Boards, they exchanged work during the busiest times of planting and harvesting.

All of the farm work required strenuous manual labor. The hay, after cutting and raking, was piled by pitchfork into small shocks. This interim step made the job of loading the loose hay onto the hay wagons easier. The space in the barn that was not needed for drying tobacco in late summer was filled with loose hay, using pitchforks to pile the hay to the roof. Additional hay was piled by hand in large stacks at the edge of the fields. After the tobacco was sold, the hay would be hauled into the barn.

The tobacco stalks were split with a long handled knife and hung on hickory or white oak sticks to wilt in the field before hanging in the barn. Three or four men were needed to hang the tobacco in tall barns.

After it was dried, stripping the tobacco was often a social event in which several neighbors or family relatives participated, partially through necessity. The dried tobacco leaves easily crumbled when handled. To prevent the crumbling, the damp tobacco, after a rain or when sprinkled with water, was stacked and covered to retain the moisture. Then, when the tobacco leaves were stripped from the stalk, they were handled rapidly to prevent drying and crumbling. The stripping was much faster when one person was assigned to each of the five or six quality grades of tobacco on each stalk. Paul, a one-man family, the Boards with one son and Joe Esker, a bachelor, coordinated their tobacco stripping projects with several neighbors.

Rosie spent her summer doing chores close to the cabin. She tended the garden, cared for the chickens and milked the cow. She carried water from the spring for cooking and cleaning. In late June and early July, she picked pails of wild blackberries. Many quarts were canned for winter pies and some berries were boiled down to jams and jellies, using a minimum amount of sugar.

The four brooding Dominique hens were each set on about a dozen fertilized eggs. The new chicks would provide additional laying hens and a few frying roosters for selling and for Sunday dinners. The old Dominique rooster that had become aggressive toward Rosie and Norbert was destined to be killed for Thanksgiving dinner.

The garden was a continuous summer project. The early garden of peas, cabbages, potatoes and green beans was harvested continuously. When a surplus accumulated, green beans, cucumbers, peppers, etc. were canned or pickled.

On a subsistence farm, the garden was a necessity. Multiplier onions and rhubarb were usually planted at the edge of the garden where they grew in their semi-wild state. They emerged as the first sign of spring shortly after the wild onions appeared in the creek bottoms. The onions, primarily eaten as green onions, were pulled from the fence row and eaten as a condiment for the bland, late winter menu of dried beans or peas and shriveled potatoes.

About half of the multiplier onions were left in the fence row unattended so they would multiply and emerge the following spring. If the weeds grew tall enough to shade the onions, a couple of swipes with a sharp briar scythe solved the problem. A large bed of table onions was planted in the garden later in the spring, using the smaller onions saved from those grown the previous year.

The rhubarb that grew early in most gardens provided a substitute for fruits that would ripen later. Like the multiplier onions, rhubarb grew without much attention. With a little sugar, the rhubarb could easily be turned into a sweet sauce for short breads, hot biscuits or tasty pies.

Before the spring plowing started, the garden and the tobacco patch were covered with manure from the barn, hauled on the farm wagon or the sled. It was spread with pitchforks to a thickness of two or three inches, covering the two areas that were critically important sources of food and income. The manure was turned under with the turning plow and the ground prepared for planting.

The garden was divided in two areas, one each for early and late gardens. Short season Bantam corn and early Jersey-Wakefield cabbages that matured in about two months were planted in the early garden. Rosie and Paul also planted garden peas, several varieties of green beans, turnips, mustard greens and tomatoes of three different varieties that matured at increasingly longer times. Cucumbers were planted in hills far apart to allow for the spreading vines. Plants of sweet, mild and hot peppers were set. Additional rows of corn were planted at two or three week intervals to provide corn throughout the summer and fall.

In the farm fields, seeds of pumpkins, squash and pole bean (usually Kentucky Wonders) were dug in between the hills of corn. Most of these long-season beans were picked dry and stored for eating in the winter.

About the first week in July, Paul and Rosie planted a late garden with many of the same vegetables. It contained additional turnips, mustard, kale and about a hundred plants of late flat Dutch cabbages for kraut and for winter storage. A row or two of late corn was planted to mature after the field corn was hard. If an early frost did not come, corn and green beans could be eaten fresh from the garden until late October.

Rosie canned much of the garden produce for eating during the winter. About a hundred quarts each of tomatoes and green beans were canned. Another hundred quarts of a combination of black-eyed peas, corn, or lima beans were canned for variety in the daily meals. The variety of produce for canning depended on the growing season and the supply of each vegetable.

Crocks of kraut and salt pickles, pickled corn and sulphered apples were stored for the winter. Dozens of smaller jars of jellies, jams, preserves and relishes were canned. A hundred or more jars of apples, peaches, cherries and blackberries were canned for cobblers, pies and deserts.

Add two or three varieties of dry beans and peas, the Irish and sweet potatoes, the onions and cabbages, the turnips and parsnips— and the survival of the family was assured until the following spring.

In the spring the wild greens appeared about the same time as the multiplier onions and the rhubarb. They provided many tasty meals. Rosie recognized and picked the edible plants: docks, thistle, plantains, pokes, dandelions, fennel, sorrel, purslane, lettuce and wild onions. The lettuce and sorrel with wild onions, when fried in bacon fat and smothered with scrambled eggs, provided a tasty breakfast dish. The poke could be boiled like asparagus when tender, and fried when the stems were larger.

Rosie usually seasoned the vegetables, whether dry beans and peas or wild greens, with a piece of salt pork. The salt pork consisted of the fat-back of a slaughtered hog. Unlike the bacon lower on the side of the hog, the salt pork was almost pure fat. It was pickled in salt brine and would keep at room temperature for months. A small piece of three or four cubic inches would season and salt a pot of vegetables. The cooked salt pork also provided a tasty morsel for the farm dog.

Most of the farms that Rosie and Paul rented had been planted with orchards as part of the food supply for the large families: apples, peaches, plums, cherries, grapes, etc. All the families planted fruit trees selectively based on their needs, their tastes, and the traditions and eating habits passed down from their ancestors.

Both Paul and Rosie's parents grew family orchards on their farms. Visits to their parents in their buggy or wagon would end with bags of apples and peaches given to them for taking home. Rosie used these fruits to can or to make a batch of apple butter. She gave several jars of apple butter to friends and relatives.

Fruit was available throughout the year. The season started at the end of May with the small, light yellow May apple. They were tasty when pan fried with a little sugar. The small red striped June apple was more tart, but equally as tasty. July and August brought the sweet apples. Even in its unripe green state, the late-summer apples were sweet, and the children preferred them for eating raw. Bushels of these apples were canned as sweet apple preserves. The children's favorite snack was a sandwich of sweet apple preserves and a thick slice of butter on a biscuit.

Fall apples (the green Horse-apple, the Maiden Blush, the Sheepnose and the Billy apple) were delicious when eaten raw or cooked in many dessert recipes. They were also canned for winter pies and dried to be reconstituted throughout the winter as fried apple pies.

The winter apples (the Stayman Winesaps and the Ben Davis) were stored in the cellar or in the barn loft under a few bundles of corn fodder to prevent freezing. The Ben Davis, a small, dark purple, almost black apple with tasty dark yellow flesh was the best winter keeper. When picked in November as a hard, immature apple, it ripened in storage, becoming mellow and tasty. These apples would keep until early spring when the weather turned warm. The plums, the peaches and the grapes were eaten raw in-season and also canned for cobblers and pies.

On the remote, abandoned farms that Paul and Rosie rented, the orchards had sometimes died or deteriorated to a nonproductive state. But there was always a generous supply of wild berries on these farms: dewberries, blackberries and wild grapes. Hazelnuts, black walnuts, and several varieties of hickory nuts were also available for those who chose to compete with the squirrels. The chestnuts that had been in plentiful supply when Rosie and Paul were teenagers had been destroyed by blight.

Ike, Paul's father, had planted a large orchard for commercial purposes when his poor health impaired his ability to work as a professional carpenter. Customers who lived within driving distance came to pick and buy fruits from Ike's orchard. When Paul was a young teenager, Ike was restricted to a wheelchair. As a hobby, with the intention to improve certain trees in the orchard, he grafted sprouts where appropriate.

Twenty years later, when the grandchildren visited Ike's orchard, many of the trees were still productive. Several trees had died and others had been broken by storms, but fruits were always available for the picking. Fruits in some form were included in every meal: fried apples, peach cobblers, plum puddings, apple preserves, gooseberry pies, jellies and jams, etc.

Insects were a constant challenge to the gardener and the orchardist. The hazards started in the garden when the seeds sprouted and peeped through the ground. The cutworm, a caterpillar of the moth, hatched in the warm garden soil and survived by eating the new sprouts at ground level. All varieties of plants were at risk in the early season.

The most effective solution to the problem was an insecticide, Paris Green. This was a poisonous arsenic compound that could be used as a powder or dissolved in water and sprayed as a liquid. The

emblem on the bag showed the skull and crossbones. Application of the insecticide on the first day the plant emerged was the ideal way to prevent cutworm destruction.

Many other insects appeared during the season: fruit flies, potato bugs, tobacco worms, cabbage worms, bean beetles and more. Most every plant had an insect to compete with the gardener. The arsenic compound was used on most of the plants. Since it could be dissolved in water, it had to be reapplied after each rain. The ideal time to apply the powder was in the early morning when the plants were wet with dew. The solubility of the powder also made it easy to wash from the vegetables before cooking and eating.

Before the first frost, the potatoes, onions, turnips and parsnips were dug and dried in a dry barn loft or attic. Then they were stored where they would not freeze during the winter. Only a few of the houses where Rosie and Paul lived had cellars or attics for storing vegetables. At other places, the root vegetables and cabbage were buried underground.

To bury the potatoes, the soil was removed to a depth of about one foot. A knoll at the top of a hill was the ideal location. A layer of fodder or hay was laid below the vegetables to protect them from the damp ground. Several bushels of potatoes would be stacked in an inverted cone shaped pile; then another layer of insulation was distributed evenly over the potatoes. The dirt from the excavation was distributed evenly over the insulation and scraps of boards or roofing were positioned to facilitate water runoff. In central Kentucky, this system could be depended on in most winters.

Cabbages were buried in a similar rectangular bed. The large heads of late flat Dutch cabbages were ideal for burying because they matured late in the fall. The plant was pulled from the ground with roots attached. The large leaves were wrapped around the head as it was placed upside-down in the ground. Insulation and dirt were mounded over the bed of cabbages to facilitate water runoff. Extremely cold weather or periods of excessive rain increased the risk to this system.

Visiting with Relatives

Rosie's two younger sisters, Sarah Marie and Jean, visited often. They walked the footpaths and dirt roads and usually visited in the afternoon to play with Norbert. Sometimes they carried a small bag of apples from their large orchard.

Two uncles and an aunt from both sides of Rosie's family lived within walking distance for an afternoon visit. Uncle Andy "Buck" Milliner and his wife, Genevieve, lived closest. They had no children. Andy was loud, flamboyant and argumentative, but also very friendly. Genevieve was an enthusiastic conversationalist. The two extroverted talkers competed continuously even when they were having conversations with others. To a small child, the constant loud arguing was unsettling.

Near their house, which sat in the woods on a west hillside, a free flowing fresh water spring ran from under the cliff. An old spring house had been built over the water source. Rosie said that this was where the Milliners distilled whiskey when it was legal, before prohibition.

Another relative, Aunt Laura Cripps, lived about the same distance as the Milliners, but in a northwesterly direction. She was Rosie's father's sister, and had married Jim Cripps. They had two children remaining at home. Florence was a teenager and Hubert, who was born blind, was seven years older than Norbert.

When visiting Aunt Laura, Florence and Hubert, Norbert's entire afternoon visit was spent playing with Hubert in the yard. Hubert had a red wagon, but because he was blind, he could neither pull or ride and guide the wagon. The only time he could play with the wagon was when other children visited, so Norbert always pulled the wagon while Hubert rode.

The greatest challenge occurred when Norbert rode in the wagon and guided as Hubert pushed. Because Norbert had never ridden in a wagon or guided, he was constantly running into things. Hubert's overly enthusiastic pushing compounded the problem. When it was time to say good-by and return home, both boys were bruised and tired but neither had blood from scrapes.

Rosie's Uncle Gilbert, her mother's youngest brother, lived a further distance to the east with his family. They had a large, two story log house that had been owned by his mother. Gilbert had attended the one-room Johnson School located in Schoolhouse Holler near a freshwater spring.

A constant supply of good water was a critical factor in the location of early homesteads and schools. The inconvenience of travel by foot, on horseback or by ox cart from these backwoods locations was of secondary importance. Isolation was an accepted condition for the early settlers.

Gilbert cared for the old farm in traditional ways similar to those of his ancestors. He replaced the old rails with new rails to maintain the fences for the livestock. When Norbert and his mother visited the family, the flock of sheep with many playful lambs was the main attraction.

Inside the large two-story log house, in the living room, a large fireplace was used for heat. At the opposite end of the room, a stairway to the upstairs bedrooms wrapped around the corner of the room. Norbert's favorite activity when inside the house was climbing three or four steps to the corner landing and jumping to the floor.

Gilbert's wife, Ursula, nicknamed Urcy, with their daughters Thelma and Mildred, visited Urcy's parents often. Her parents lived on a hill farm near Clifty Creek south of the Whitfill farm where Rosie and Paul lived.

Urcy's sister, Cora, invited the neighborhood women to a quilting party. Aunt Genevieve walked the footpath through the woods and joined Rosie and Norbert for the walk to the party.

The quilt top, the cotton batting and the cotton sheet bottom were arranged in three layers. They were attached to the wooden quilt frames that hung from the ceiling in the living room. The frame with the quilt parts was lowered to a convenient height for the women sitting in the straight backed, splint bottomed chairs.

With their needles and threads, and with thimbles on their middle finger, they pushed the needles through the three quilt pieces. They sewed the layers together following the fancy patterns in the quilt pieces in the quilt top. The women who sat on two sides of the frame progressed toward the center. As they completed each area, the quilt was wound onto the quilt frames until the women met in the center, completing the sewing.

The party ended with a small bowl of blackberry cobbler with sweet cream topping and a cup of coffee or milk. The afternoon of conversation, laughter and productive fun ended early with adequate time for the women to return home for supper with their families.

Visiting Grandpa Clark

During the summer, Paul made periodic trips to visit his parents at the community of Mount Hebron, taking Norbert with him. Traveling the footpaths through the woods was a two-mile walk. Along the way, when climbing the steep hills, Norbert would became tired and ask to ride on Paul's back. When they reached the top of the hill near Frazier Given's house, Norbert again walked.

They passed the small Saint Francis Catholic Church at Mount Hebron. Paul would always check the front door and, if it was unlocked, they entered for a visit. The church was a small replica of the larger St. Paul Church that they attended most Sundays. It contained a few stained glass windows and a small altar with a crucifix and spires. The altar was about the same size as the side altars in the large St. Paul church.

After visiting the church, they changed direction to visit a sawmill so Paul could inquire about buying a few boards to build a new box for the farm sled. When they approached the noisy sawmill powered by a steam engine, the operator shut the sawmill down. Jess Whitten, owner of the sawmill, was a neighborhood friend. Jess pulled his file from his pocket and began filing the large circular saw blade while talking to Paul.

Without warning, Jess decided to entertain Paul and Norbert by blowing the steam whistle. Under the full pressure of the steam boiler, the whistle sounded deafening instead of entertaining. Norbert, who had never heard a steam whistle, climbed Paul's leg to escape. Jess was embarrassed to the extent that he tried to apologize to Norbert by giving him a nickel.

Paul and Norbert returned down the dirt road past the church and then over the hill to visit Ike and Janie. This time, Ike was lying in his bed, gaunt and sickly. His wheelchair sat beside his bed but he did not get up. He spoke to Norbert, remembering his name, and reached out his hand to him. Norbert was scared. It was the first time he had seen someone in this sickly condition.

Later in the summer, the family decided to attend Mass at St. Francis Church on Sunday morning and then spend the remainder of the day visiting with Ike and Janie. Mass was celebrated there about once a month or when a funeral occurred.

The shortest distance to the church was by a footpath through the woods. Several barbed wire fences and a few wire gates were obstacles to be manipulated along the way.

When they reached the church, several people usually were in attendance. Horses hitched to farm wagons and horses with saddles were tied to trees in the church yard. A couple of cars also sat in the churchyard at the edge of the dirt road.

When the family entered the church, the congregation was standing and it was obvious that the Clarks had arrived late. The family walked slowly down the center isle looking for a seat large enough for the three of them. About half-way to the front they found a partially vacant pew. They genuflected and entered the pew aware of stares from the congregation. The sermon was already finished and the Priest was preparing for the offertory. The walk from the cabin to the church had clearly taken longer than anticipated.

Janie, Paul's mother, was in the congregation and greeted the family after Mass. They walked down the hill to the Clark house where Norbert played in the yard to avoid meeting Grandpa Ike in his sickbed. When dinner was ready and Norbert was called to eat, he ran through the living room to the kitchen ignoring Ike. They started home in the afternoon in time to feed the pig and chickens, gather the eggs and milk the cow.

Andy's Surprise

Rosie's brother, Andy William, made a surprise visit one summer day. He had been incarcerated in the Eddyville prison in western Kentucky for two years as a punishment for making moonshine whiskey. Andy had bought a new pair of Duckhead overalls at the Big

7 Mercantile Store when he got off the bus in Leitchfield. He walked the back roads to visit Rosie, his next older sister. After lunch, he said good-by, beginning his walk on the additional two or more miles home. Then, after just a few minutes, Andy returned to the cabin, smelling strongly of skunk odor. As he'd walked the path through the woods, he surprised a skunk that had been digging for grubs in a rotten hollow stump. The surprised skunk jumped out of the hollow stump and sprayed the foul smelling fluid on Andy. Since he was not far from the cabin, Andy returned to ask Rosie's help in solving the problem.

They heated a drum of water to wash Andy's clothes and Rosie convinced Andy to take a bath in the kitchen. He was given a can of tomatoes to smear on his face and arms, which had been exposed to the skunk fluid. Tomato juice was the traditional method for neutralizing the skunk odor. Paul gave Andy clothes to wear while his clothes were washed and dried, but they were much too small for Andy. The pants reached only about halfway between his knees and his feet. The shirt was so small that half the buttons at the chest could not be buttoned. Barefooted, with the Ichabod Crane look, Andy was a comical character.

Andy's clothes were washed in lye soap with a second wash in the tomatoes. After rinsing, his clothes were hung on the clothesline to dry. Rosie convinced Andy to stay overnight to allow time for his clothes to dry. The strong soapy water with the tomato rinse had solved the problem and Andy continued his journey home after breakfast the next morning.

Fall Chores

The late summer progressed on schedule. When the ears of corn matured and the shucks turned brown, the corn fodder, still green, was topped above the drooping ears. The corn fodder would be a substitute for hay for the calf, the milk cow and the horses through the winter.

The black eyed peas and the white navy beans were picked, dried, shelled and hung from the ceiling in flour sacks in the kitchen. The onions and the potatoes including the sweet potatoes were dug and stored temporarily in the barn loft to dry. Before freezing temperatures arrived, the new vegetables would be moved to the attic of the log cabin.

The corn crop had been so productive that Paul decided to raise a litter of pigs for extra money. The few extra frying roosters and the old hens culled from the flock would provide meat for the winter. A fifty pound can of lard, bought at Drake's store, would be used for shortening.

Paul also decided to keep the heifer calf to grow into another milk cow. The calf was one-half Jersey and would produce rich, saleable cream and a fat veal calf for market. At about four months old, the calf was removed from the milk cow and taken to Joe Esker's home farm for weaning. She would join half a dozen heifers that he was keeping as replacements for a few old cows.

It was increasingly obvious that the new team of young draft horses would not grow into an acceptable farm team. The larger gelding, even-tempered Dock, worked tirelessly, as if he accepted the hum-drum nature of the daily labor as his destiny in life. But the smaller, high spirited filly, Nippy, was upset to the point of panic by the most insignificant movements. A bird flying from a fencepost beside the road caused sudden and unpredictable reactions. She might jerk the sled spilling a load of rocks or a load of poles on the way to the woodpile. Her over-excitable nature could sometimes urge the dull, half-trained gelding into a state of immature behavior.

Opossum Hunters

As fall progressed, the corn was gathered and the fodder stacked beside the barn. The leaves fell from the trees and late green beans and corn were frozen by the frost. One night after supper Paul mentioned that the "opossums might have found the ripe persimmons." About one quarter mile northeast of the house, near the spring branch, several mature, productive persimmon trees were growing. "Before we go to bed, we'll take the dog and the lantern and see if there are any opossums in those trees," Paul said to Norbert.

Before they started the adventurous journey into the cool night, they found their warm winter coats and filled the lantern with kerosene. They gave the opossums plenty of time to venture from their dens. Then Paul and Norbert, carrying the lantern and a burlap bag and accompanied by the over enthusiastic dog, Spot, started down the hill towards the persimmon trees.

When they were half way to the trees, the dog, who had run ahead, was already barking. With the light from the lantern and the moon rising in the east, they could see the forms of three large opossums. Holding the lantern above their heads, they could see the opossums' beady eyes shining in the dark.

Norbert's first question was "How do we get the opossums out of the trees?" Paul answered, "We will have to climb the trees!"

The dog barked impatiently under the trees, jumping high on the tree trunks as if he was trying to climb to get the opossums. Norbert held the lantern high so Paul could climb the tree to a limb above the first opossum. While holding to the body of the tree, he shook the limb underneath him with his foot until the opossum lost its grip and fell to the ground. A shower of ripe persimmons fell to the ground around Norbert and the dog.

Spot immediately grabbed the opossum, which went into a seemingly lifeless state, its natural defense mechanism. While Norbert and the dog watched the opossum, Paul climbed down from the tree. He picked up the silent opossum by its long boney tail and dropped it into the burlap bag. While Norbert held the lantern and the burlap bag that contained the opossum, the procedure was duplicated up two other trees producing a total of three large opossums.

Back at the cabin, Paul decided to wait until morning to kill and skin the opossums. They were placed under the wash tub on wide wooden boards so they could not dig out. A large heavy stone was placed on the tub. Norbert went to sleep thinking about the opossums, and in the morning, he was up early. He dressed and ran out the door to see if the opossums were still under the tub. They were.

After breakfast, Paul killed the opossums by breaking their necks, being careful not to damage the pelts. When the pelt was removed, it was stretched over a thin wooden board that had been rounded and pointed on one end to fit the exact shape of the pelt. Any fat that remained on the skin was scraped off with a dull knife, again being careful not to damage the skin. The skins were allowed to cure for a few weeks hanging from nails on the side of the barn where the sun would speed the process. After removing the pelts from the boards and reversing the skins so the fur was outside, Paul sold the pelts at Sam Terry's hardware store in Big Clifty. The price received for each pelt was equal to a day's farm wage.

The meaty carcasses of the opossums seemed too promising to waste. Rosie had never cooked an opossum, but after a discussion with Paul, they decided to remove some of the legs and fry them like chicken legs. During the frying process, both were surprised that the amount of grease in the skillet doubled. The opossums, like all hibernating animals, accumulated large amounts of fat in their muscle tissue to survive the cold months in winter hibernation.

The fried opossum legs were soft and slick and spongy. Even the dog, always adequately fed with scraps from the table, refused the pan-fried morsels. Neither Paul nor Rosie knew the southern gourmet recipe of opossum stuffed with sweet potatoes.

Sammy Is Born

On November 3, 1940, Rosie gave birth to their second son. He was named Samuel Thomas, traditional names in the Clark ancestry. Paul's mother, Janie, midwife for all the families in that corner of the country, came to the house overnight to help with the delivery. Francis, Rosie's sister who had recently finished elementary school, was brought to the house to stay the ten days that Rosie was to rest in bed after the birth. Mary Alta, Rosie's mother, and youngest sisters, Sarah Marie and Jean, visited to see the new baby. Frances did the cooking and took care of the baby. Paul helped with the washing, hauling and heating the water.

7

EARNING A LITTLE MORE MONEY

Cash in the City

Paul and Joe Esker, working with the neighbors, finished their farm work earlier in the fall than most farmers. They had enough tobacco among them to provide an adequate truck load for Wavy Drake, the local truck driver. Wavy, the only truck owner in the neighborhood, did all the hauling of grain, livestock, and tobacco. He also hauled farm equipment, fertilizer and coal for those who burned coal.

Paul decided to go to Louisville with Wavy, hoping that he might get a job at the Seventh Street Tobacco Warehouse, where tobacco was sold by auction. It was then processed for storage in large wooden hogsheads and aged until needed in the cigarette manufacturing industry. By arriving early, shortly after the warehouse had opened, the possibility of getting a job was greater, since most farmers were still preparing their tobacco for the market.

Rosie and Norbert would care for the chickens, the pig, the milk cow and the horses. If help was needed, Rosie could call on Joe Esker or her brothers.

Paul did get a job. He worked five days a week, sometimes long days because the timing of the farm trucks was unpredictable. During the week he paid board to stay with the family of his brother Francis or with Rosie's sister Theresa's family. He rode the city bus to and from work.

On Friday evenings, Paul rode the Kentucky bus line home to Grayson County. The bus left downtown Louisville at five p.m. for a trip of about 75 miles that took three hours over crooked roads, stopping at several small towns.

At the Big Clifty bus stop, site of a small greasy-spoon restaurant and hang-out, Paul sometimes connected and found a ride with someone from down the St. Paul ridge. At other times he walked the five or six miles to home. He always walked the last two miles to the cabin since these roads were impassible by car.

On Sunday afternoon, Paul left home early with enough time to walk the long distance to the bus station. Most of the time, a passerby gave Paul a ride.

Weekend Responsibilities

On the weekend, Paul took Rosie's eggs and cream to market. He also took a few burlap bags of ear corn to the mill at the same time, so there would be crushed corn for the milk cow and the heifer calf. High protein feeds were bought and fed as supplements to the plentiful supply of crushed corn, promoting higher production of both cream and eggs. At home, Paul also cut a week's supply of firewood for heating and cooking.

On one weekend during the winter, after a light snowfall, Paul and Rosie prepared as usual for a trip to the mill. Paul filled several bags with ear corn while Rosie prepared the eggs and the cream. The two gallon stainless steel pail, especially purchased for the cream, was filled. A case of thirty dozen eggs, each egg cushioned in its individual pocket, was filled. The extra hens, hatched the previous spring, had just begun to lay eggs. Three or four additional dozens of eggs were cushioned in the bottom of a hickory-splint basket.

The farm sled, with its new box built with lumber from Jess Whiten's sawmill, was prepared for the trip. Several bags of ear corn were loaded. The young team of excited horses was slowly hitched with constant, low, calming commands of "Whoa - - Whoa!"

They proceeded slowly toward the cabin. The horses pranced and shied nervously at the blowing snow that their hooves were stirring into the wind. Stopping at the cabin, the cream and the eggs were loaded, nestled in the corner of the sled between the bags of corn.

Norbert would usually have accompanied Paul on the trip to the mill. They would take the sled to Joe Esker's barn, where they would transfer the produce to the farm wagon and continue the trip to the mill. But, because of the cold weather and the spirited behavior of the young team, Norbert was not allowed on this trip.

Norbert pulled a chair to the high kitchen window by the water bucket and watched Paul standing in the sled. The team started fast but under control and slowed to a steady pace. The loaded sled was easy to pull on the new snow. When they reached the shallow spring branch that flowed from the hillside and trickled across the road, the team stopped. On trips before the snow fell, they had crossed the stream without hesitation.

Paul urged the team to continue across the water but they refused. With additional encouragement from Paul, they reared and swung sideways endangering the sled and its contents. Paul dismounted from the sled. He attempted to calm the team by talking quietly and rubbing their muzzles. Holding their bridles, he straightened the team with the sled and prepared to drive from the ground.

Stepping on the side of the road into the briars and bushes, Paul had apparently stepped too close to a large covey of quail. The quail exploded loudly, flying barely above the heads of the already nervous team. The surprised team reared straight into the air and leaped across the stream, clearing the water and then galloping down the rough dirt road. Paul was able to hold onto the reins and run beside the sled, bounding over rocks, bushes and briars until the team tired.

Several bags of corn had bounced off the sled. The case of eggs and the cream had bounced off and the loose eggs in the basket were broken.

Norbert, watching the action from the kitchen window, alerted his mother. Grabbing their coats, they both ran down the road toward the spring branch to help Paul pick up the pieces. Then Paul turned the team around and headed back to the cabin. The team shied cautiously and hesitated but crossed the stream without incident. As they passed the briar patch from which the covey of quail had exploded, their ears were at alert and they snorted nervously.

The top of the cream can, inserted deeply into the pail, had remained in place. The pail had only a minor dent and the cream was protected. The bags of corn that had bounced off the sled were unharmed.

The highly cushioned case of thirty dozen eggs had popped open when it bounced from the sled, so several eggs in the top layers were broken along with the eggs in the basket. Rosie and Paul washed the unbroken eggs and returned them to the egg case. On the second stream crossing, the young team crossed cautiously, stepping lightly through the shallow water.

Catastrophe Strikes a Neighbor

On another weekend that winter, Paul returned to Grayson County on the Kentucky Bus Line. A neighbor, Shelton Denis, who also had a job for the winter in Louisville, was riding the bus with Paul. A winter snowstorm was beginning, slowing the bus.

The restaurant at Big Clifty was still open. There, a friend of Paul's, Roy Drake, offered Paul and Shelton a ride down St. Paul ridge before the winter storm became too severe. Paul accepted the ride but Shelton decided to wait for a friend who usually met him at the restaurant. Roy dropped Paul off at Hickorynut Corner, near the west end of St. Paul Road, from which he could walk the two miles across the holler to his family.

The next morning, someone knocked at the door of the cabin and asked Paul about his friend Shelton, who had not yet returned home. Later in the day, another stranger knocked at the door. This man, who could have been the sheriff or his deputy, had a long talk with Paul concerning Shelton.

Shelton had been found nearly frozen to death under a snowdrift, an empty whiskey bottle in his pocket. Paul explained that it was convenient for workers to cash their checks at the whiskey store and that most, including himself, bought a bottle of whiskey when they cashed their checks. Efforts to revive Shelton failed. He had a wife and three small children who suffered the loss of their father.

Paul Seeks a Neighbor's Help

In late winter, the supply of wood was nearly exhausted. Paul, working in Louisville during the week and busy with the weekend chores, could not find time to cut more wood. A neighbor, Frazier Givens, agreed to cut wood for Paul.

Paul borrowed Joe Esker's farm wagon to haul the wood. He drove the team and wagon to the woods on the hill north of Frazier's bottomland on Clifty Creek and was surprised to find the oak wood split and neatly stacked in four ricks. A rick, which sold for two dollars, filled the wagon. Paul bought and hauled the four ricks anticipating that he would have enough wood, including wood for the cook stove, to last until the following winter.

He could easily split the straight grained oak into the smaller sticks needed for the cook stove. So, when Paul next saw Frazier, he said: "This must have been a tall straight tree, big enough for saw logs and lumber."

Frazier's reply: "When you take the time to cut the logs; haul them to the mill; return to the mill to haul the lumber home; pay the sawyer who sawed the lumber—if you don't have a serious need for the lumber, it is more profitable to sell the logs as firewood."

After thinking about the Frazier's answer, Paul kicked at the dead leaves and responded, "I see your point. The difference between paying someone to saw the logs; not considering the time involved; and the eight dollars in your pocket, could be several dollars." Simple farmer's logic was expressed in both answers.

In the spring, Paul exchanged the spirited filly, Nippy, for a gelding. He traveled to Crow Holler east of West Clifty and Clarkson and traded with the farmer who had raised both horses. For an extra twenty-five dollars, Paul got a gelding that matched his first gelding better in color, size and temperament. The two horses remained a team that worked with Paul for sixteen years.

THE COLD, COLD SNOWDRIFT: SHEL'S GRAVE

(for Shelton Dennis)

Shel went to sleep beneath the cold, cold snowdrift.
Shel went to sleep, his bottle by his side.
Shel went to sleep beneath the cold, cold snowdrift
And they found him there next morning where he died.

Shel was a friendly, kind, warmhearted fellow.
He loved his family, worked his job and saved.
But the bottle in his pocket was his downfall.
It dimmed his mind; the snow-drift was his grave.

Just a mile or more from home, the warm fire burning,
They waited for their Shel, then went to bed.
They slept warmly while the cold wind blew the snowdrift,
And they found him there next morning; Shel was dead.

Shel had a loving wife, three little children
Standing by the cold, cold grave that day.
Their tears were quickly frozen in the snowdrift,
The cold, cold snow that took their Shel away.

- Song by Norbert Clark

8
LIVING WITH
THE LANDLORD

Log Cabin to Farmhouse

The following spring, Joe Esker decided to turn the Whitfill farm where Rosie and Paul lived into pasture land. He would cultivate his more level and productive home farm. Paul and Rosie planted their garden at this new farm and slowly moved everything from the log cabin to the more modern farm house.

The yard was bordered by a white, painted slat picket fence. Several silver poplar shade trees grew in the yard. A bored well had been dug by the kitchen door and a well house had been built. A windlass was used to wind a rope onto a round wooden spool lifting the well bucket filled with water.

The white weather boarded house had four large rooms in an "L" shape. Two large screened porches provided storage and working areas throughout the year. Joe Esker moved his furniture and belongings into two rooms. Paul, Rosie and their children would occupy the other two rooms and they would share the porches.

The smokehouse for curing and storing meat was weatherproof. The chicken house with both roosting and laying sections and a small brooder house were already enclosed in tall wire fences. The garden was also fenced to stop rabbits from eating the plants. Three fenced lots around the barn were designed to hold pigs or calves or a milk cow for morning milking. The brood mare with a new colt could also be separated from the work horses.

A loading chute for driving market animals into the truck was attached to the side of the barn. The chute opened to stalls inside the barn. The large corncrib, with a shed long enough to shelter the buggy and farm wagon, stood in the corner of the barn lot. A large pond was dug in another corner.

A manual corn sheller with a long crank and a large flywheel was used to shell corn for the chickens. Norbert was able to shell the corn if he sped up the flywheel before he put the corn in the chute. When the flywheel was turning at high speed, he could shell a half bushel of corn, enough to feed the chickens for a few days. Joe Esker's farm was not a plantation, but over the years, he had incorporated many conveniences.

Rosie took over the household duties. She cooked and sewed, cleaned and washed clothes, canned and preserved the fruits and vegetables. Joe Esker and Paul helped when needed, milking the cow, picking fruit and vegetables and digging potatoes. With a generous supply of water, Rosie found it was much easier to clean the linoleum floors, wash clothes, dishes and children. Cooking on the large cook stove with larger burners, a warming oven and a hot water reservoir made the job easier and more efficient. The oven with the round thermometer produced more consistent quality in the biscuits and pies.

Joe Esker seemed to like the arrangement. He ate and mingled with the family continuously. He enjoyed taking Norbert and Samuel to the barn to see a new calf or a new litter of pigs. When he went to town or to the store, he always bought a small bag of candy orange slices for Samuel and Norbert. He subscribed to a magazine that Rosie enjoyed and shared his Courier Journal newspaper with Paul.

Norbert, who was learning his letters and numbers, went through the newspaper with his mother finding and identifying letters and numbers. Many times Joe Esker left the newspaper lying on the table open to the stock market news with many columns of small numbers. These mysterious pages were interesting to Norbert who could find dozens of any number in the columns.

A typical day started at daylight at the barn feeding the livestock. The work horses that were turned out to pasture at night were brought into the barn, fed a hearty breakfast of ear corn and then harnessed. The milk cow that had been separated in one of the small lots the night before was fed and milked.

By the time the morning chores were finished, Rosie had the breakfast on the table. The breakfast always included some meat: pork sausage, bacon, smoked ham or shoulder. Eggs in some form were always plentiful. Hot biscuits and brown gravy, home canned jellies and preserves and home churned butter were always part of breakfast.

Joe Esker liked to start the workday each morning after breakfast with his "eye-opener." A tea kettle of hot water was always heating on the cook stove and Joe Esker kept a keg of moonshine whiskey in a large trunk in his bedroom. When the keg was empty, he took it to the moonshiner to be refilled. A smaller keg with a spigot, set on the trunk for convenience, was filled by siphoning whiskey from the larger keg. A glass tumbler to which a teaspoon of sugar had been added was filled about one third full with the hot water from the teakettle. A double shot of the moonshine whiskey was added to the hot, sweet water and mixed. Two glasses were prepared, one each for

Joe Esker and Paul. The tasty "eye-opener" was gulped down in two swallows as they walked out the door toward the barn and the fields.

That morning "eye-opener" before starting work in the field was the only time Joe Esker was seen to drink whiskey. The old trunk, which passed into Rosie and Paul's possession when Joe Esker sold the farm, still smelled of the whiskey 70 years later.

A Sample of Real Farm Life

The summer at Joe Esker's farm was filled with adventure for an inquisitive four-year old. When he was not permitted to go to the fields with the men, Norbert spent his time helping his mother or caring for his younger brother, Samuel.

One of his favorite pastimes was riding the pedal-driven grindstone on the screened-in porch. Norbert's legs were not long enough to follow the pedals through their complete revolution. But with an energetic push on the pedal, the centrifugal motion of the heavy sandstone wheel returned the opposite pedal. Norbert could then reach the pedal again and give another shove. He could build speed with the alternate pushing strategy and watch the wheel turn for several minutes. Sometimes he would fill the pint sized tin can above the grindstone with water. He could adjust the spigot from a slow drip to a continuous stream. Although he was forbidden to sharpen kitchen knives, he could sharpen wooden sticks or experiment with stones.

Joe Esker had a push mower. Norbert was not strong enough to mow the grass, but he could turn the mower upside down and pretend to mow the entire lawn.

The young colt in one of the barn lots with the broodmare provided additional entertainment. When Norbert raked a tobacco stick rapidly across the woven wire fence, the colt reacted to the noise with energetic running and bucking.

The loud, bass toned bullfrogs in the grass around the pond remained quiet when Norbert came near. But if he backed away near the fence and remained quiet, they would again start their loud croaking. Norbert could see them in the grass in the shallow water and watch their white throats expand and contract like small balloons as they croaked. If he ran around the pond croaking like the frogs, many of the frogs that he had not seen jumped from the grass into the pond.

Sheep-Killing Dogs

Several more interesting events filled Norbert's summer. One day at noon, the dog, Spot, alerted the family that three neighborhood farmers were approaching the house. At the yard-gate they stopped, looking intently at the dog still inside the yard fence. He stopped barking and started wagging his tail as a friendly greeting.

The man who seemed to be the most interested in the dog was Rosie's uncle, Gilbert Milliner, so Paul and Joe Esker went outside and greeted the small group. Then they knelt and looked at the dog as they were instructed by Gilbert Milliner.

After a few minutes of discussion, Paul returned to the house, went into the bedroom and came out carrying his shotgun. Rosie interrupted and asked what was happening. Paul explained that the men were searching for the dogs that had killed Gilbert's sheep. Spot had blood on his muzzle, seemingly clear evidence that he was guilty. It was an unwritten law among the farmers that sheep-killing dogs would be killed. Paul was loading the gun to carry out the sentence.

Rosie started to laugh. She explained that on the previous day, she had walked through the school house holler with the boys to visit Iva, Paul's sister. The dog had gone with them. For lunch, Iva had opened a can of beet pickles, pouring the purple beet juice out the kitchen door. The dog, anticipating scraps from the table, had rushed to the doorstep and Iva had poured the beet juice on the dog's head.

Paul took Rosie outside to explain the story to the men. Upon closer examination, they all agreed that the purple color on the dog's head was not blood. After a hearty laugh, everyone agreed to the happy ending of a potentially sad story.

Unexplained Darkness

On another morning, Joe Esker knocked on Paul and Rosie's bedroom door. They were usually out of bed and in the kitchen caring for the boys when Joe Esker awoke, so Joe explained that his clock alarm had sounded and it was time to get up. Although surprised, Paul and Rosie arose, got dressed and started attending to their routine tasks.

After breakfast it was still dark outside. Joe Esker found yesterday's newspaper and searched for the prediction of an eclipse. They could not understand why it was dark when the clock said that it should be light. What event might have darkened the sun or slowed the rotation of the earth?

At about this time, a half mile to the east, they saw two or three dim lights slowly crossing the field at the edge of the woods. They knew that these were the lanterns carried by the workmen who walked this path every morning to catch the train that took them to their jobs repairing the railroad tracks.

This triggered an investigation of the clock. Because the alarm had sounded earlier, the clock had not been suspected. They soon came to the conclusion that the alarm setting must have accidently been changed. The mystery of darkness when there should have been light was solved.

Joe Langley's Beehives

Another bachelor, named Joe Langley, lived in the holler northwest of Joe Esker's farm. He had an orchard of several apple trees that ripened throughout the summer. He also had a few bee hives that he had constructed using hollow logs about two feet tall. The bees constructed their honey combs by fastening them to the cross sticks that were installed at different heights in the hollow logs.

Joe harvested the honey according to a seasonal schedule. The honey in the comb was cut from the hive in sections and stored in fifty pound metal lard cans. At the point of the summer when most of the community's molasses had been consumed, he sold his honey in the comb to his neighbors, giving them a very low price because it might contain a stray ant or a piece of tree bark which could be easily removed.

One day, Paul and Norbert rode a workhorse to visit Joe Langley. Because Old Joe Langley reminded Norbert of "Old Joe Clark", a tune that Paul played on his fiddle, he hummed the tune all the way to Joe's farm. Paul bought enough honey from Old Joe to fill the lard pail he had brought with him, about one gallon.

Joe mentioned that a couple of his apple trees were full with a generous crop almost ready to be picked. Paul ate one of the apples as a test and promised to return in a week or two with burlap bags. Paul was familiar with the culture and quality of apples because he'd grown up caring for a large orchard of many varieties on his father's farm.

75

Joe Esker's small orchard was mostly summer apples and a few ancient peach trees. A few untrimmed grape vines hung over the garden fence. As a bachelor, the orchard and garden were only of secondary importance to Joe Esker.

At the Clark home, much of the honey in the comb was eaten as a snack, the way people today eat candy bars. The liquid honey that drained from the comb was eaten at breakfast on corn fritters or biscuits. Rosie sometimes prepared a snack for the hungry Clark boys, a sandwich of honey and butter on biscuits left over from breakfast.

Little Grandma Milliner

Late in the summer Rosie's grandmother, called Marcella, Marty or Little Grandma Milliner, visited for an extended time. In her eighties she was spry and energetic. She helped Rosie with the children, all the housework, the cooking and the canning. When helping Rosie peel and can peaches from the old Red Indian peach tree, she found that the small peaches, dark red in color with small black spots, contained several worms. Rosie fretted about the waste and the worms. Marty's response was "The worms are peaches too. They eat nothing but peaches."

Little Grandma had arrived at the Clark household carrying her necessities in a pillowcase. In the absence of social programs or a pension, Marty lived with her relatives. She also carried a bag of quilt pieces that she sewed when not involved with housework. The quilts were gifts for her grandchildren as they married.

Marty was also an avid conversationalist. Norbert liked to sit nearby and listen to the stories. He showed the same interest that he displayed when his mother read books aloud to him.

Once Marty told a story about a panther that ate some kittens. 'Panther' was the local name for the cougar or mountain lion native to the area when she had been a child. The story described the time when Marty had just finished elementary school. She had been asked to babysit for a farm family at Beaver Dam Creek. The mother of the family had given birth to a new baby and was required to stay in bed for ten days. Marty was hired to stay with the family for the entire time. She cooked, took care of the children, washed and ironed as the mother would have done. She also gathered vegetables from the garden, fed the chickens and gathered their eggs.

As well, Marty took care of a mother cat with kittens, turning them out several times during the day and at bedtime. One night when it was time for the cats to come back inside, one of the kittens did not return. Another night, a second kitten could not be found and large tracks like those of a 'panther' were found in the dust. On yet another night, a third kitten was attacked. This time the mother cat found courage to fight the intruder, causing a loud commotion of growls and meows. The father of the family quickly grabbed his gun from the rack over the door of the cabin. He fired a shot in the direction of the noise. The 'panther' ran away and the kitten was saved.

Civil War Stories

Marty, who was born in 1858, remembered the Civil War. She told stories about the experiences of the local families during the war, including a story about one of her neighbors whom she called "a deserter." The man had lived in a shelter under a cliff near Clifty Creek during the war. He returned home after dark to see the family and instruct them about the work that was needed to maintain the farm. "He was a deserter," she said. "If he had been caught, he would have been shot, but I don't blame him. He had a family to care for and he just did not have the fifty dollars to buy a deferment like some other men did. He did the right thing!"

Marty remembered Civil War troops passing near her home and then camping for weeks by the fresh water springs nearby. She said that they built log or "corduroy" roads through the muddy area and that the "Bump—Bump—Bump" of wagons on the road could be heard for days on end. The troops stole the farmers' livestock and burned rail fences in their campfires.

"Mr. Johnson had just split new rails and built new fences around his farm. Those lazy scoundrels burned his new rails in their campfires. The whole forest was around them but they were too lazy to cut the wood."

Both Union and Confederate troops travelled through the area because the Salt River Road near Marty's home had been a major north-south road dating back to the time of the Indians. The courthouse in Leitchfield was burned by the Confederates in 1864, when Marty was six years old.

About a hundred years later, in the early 1960s, a farmer digging a pond in a field beside the Salt River Road, uncovered split logs buried in the ground. They were thought to have been part of the corduroy road built by the civil war troops around a low muddy spot in the road.

When Little Grandma's visit ended, we really missed her part in our home.

Door to Door Salesgirls

Later in the summer, three neighborhood girls came to the house. One was Rosie's first cousin, Mary Rose Conder and the other two girls were Thelma and Mildred Langley, daughters of Willie and Bessie Langley who lived near Clifty Creek on Salt River Road. The girls were selling salves, lotions and powders, participating in a mail-order program in which they could earn premiums such as purses and cameras. By working as a team and combining orders under one name, they could earn more premiums and share them. They were carrying a box Brownie camera which they had earned.

After Rosie had ordered boxes of Rosebud Salve and face powder, the girls asked to take a picture of Norbert and his dog, Spot. Rosie insisted that Norbert change into a new sailor suit that she had ordered from the Sears Roebuck catalog. She had planned that Norbert would wear the new suit to the church picnic and the county fair. Rosie, Norbert and the girls found a sunny spot in the corner of the pasture field east of the barn. The girls delivered the picture a few weeks later along with the Rosebud Salve.

Celebrating the Church Picnic

Norbert did wear his sailor suit to the church picnic. Since Joe Esker had sold his surrey and the team of classy horses, the trip to the church was made in the farm wagon pulled by the team of young work horses.

When they arrived at the church grounds and hitched the horses to a tree, many other teams had already arrived. A few cars were parked on the west lawn.

The crowd was gathering on the east side of the church around the two-room school house. Rosie and Paul with Norbert and Samuel were immediately met and welcomed by relatives and friends. A group of musicians on a stage was already playing. The band was led by a young fiddle player, Herman Alvey. He played the same square dance hoedowns that Paul played, and also the same Irish jigs, hornpipes and reels traditional to the area. Herman's sister sang the popular country music songs. Most of the audience had heard these songs on their battery radios or their record players. Since the musicians had no electricity or amplifiers, the sounds of the music did not extend far into the crowd.

The women of the parish had prepared and cooked all the food at home and transported it to the picnic. The eating area with the food was isolated from the crowd by a chicken-wire fence nailed to the posts. The tables were rough lumber platforms nailed to posts that the men had dug into the ground the day before.

Other men of the parish had gathered at the church grounds the previous day to kill the sheep for the featured dish, the traditional mutton. A rope was tied around the sheep's neck. The sheep was laid on its side, its neck extending over a heavy block of wood. A sharp ax was aimed precisely behind the sheep's ears and swung strongly to cut the head off in one clip. With ropes on the rear legs, the sheep was immediately hung to bleed. It was later skinned, cleaned of entrails and cut into pieces that fit into large black iron kettles. The meat was boiled over open fires until tender and then taken home by the men to bake in their kitchen ovens. The meat brought to the picnic dinner was sliced and ready to serve. The quality and size of the slices varied greatly because the men were neither butchers nor cooks.

Many pans of fried chicken were also served. Iron kettles of green beans (Kentucky Wonders and tender Half-Runners) sat at the end of the tables. Chicken and dumplings, dried white navy beans and black-eyed peas were in generous supply for the dinner. Pan pies, cakes and cobblers made with fruits from the home-orchards were plentiful.

Norbert in his new sailor suit ate dinner with his mother. Rosie's younger sisters and cousins had taken possession of young Samuel as their live doll. Sarah Maria and Jean, Rosie's youngest sisters, and Mary Ann and Betty, her first cousins, argued among themselves about whose turn it was to carry Samuel. Paul had been scheduled to work in one of the concessions.

Norbert's favorite dish at the dinner was the green beans. The large, black pot of tender, sweet Half-Runners was about one-third field corn, cut from the cob and cooked with the beans. Hot green peppers had also been finely diced and cooked in the beans. The small pieces of hot green pepper that clung to the tongue were not hot enough to discourage Norbert. Rosie returned twice to get more of the green beans for Norbert. On the third trip, she returned with an empty plate. "No more green beans! We will have to ask the old Indian lady for the recipe."

Norbert's interest was aroused. Rosie had read stories and showed Norbert pictures of Indians, so he questioned Rosie about where they lived. She said that they lived nearby on the road to the cemetery.*

The picnic continued, and after lunch Norbert asked to go to the toilet. The men's toilet was on the south side of St. Paul Road, in the woods. The undergrowth in the woods, the bushes, the briars and the vines hid the toilet from view. The smelly toilet used by the large

---

* *This story about the Indians remained in my memory. When I started studying American History in the 5th or 6th grade, I asked Mother about the Indians. She said that they had moved from the parish. Years later, in 2006, on the way to the cemetery to visit the graves of my parents, I remembered the Indians when we passed the farm where they had lived. A neighbor, Mike Darst, was sitting on his front porch. He would have been a teenager when the Indians lived there. I stopped to talk to him, asking about the Indians. "Yes", he said, "the old Indians lived there when I was a teenager. Their names were…" His memory lapsed and he could not recall their names. My other attempts to learn their names have also failed.*

crowd had overflowed, so Norbert was instructed to go into the woods behind the toilet.

The ride home in the afternoon in the farm wagon was dull compared to the excitement of the picnic.

The Parade and County Fair

Norbert also wore his sailor suit to the county fair at Leitchfield on the day that it opened. The opening of the fair was preceded by a parade that started at the court house and ended at the fairgrounds on the north edge of the city. After the long journey from home on the dirt roads, Paul hitched the horses with the farm wagon to a hitching rail near the train depot. After walking the two city blocks from the depot to the shade of a large maple tree beside the street where the parade would pass, they sat in the shade and ate fried chicken with the biscuits and milk they had brought from home.

The crowd and the excitement grew as the parade proceeded northward, passing St. Joseph's Church and the shade tree under which they waited. Marching bands and horses were joined by farm wagons and ox carts filled with men and women dressed in historical clothing. It was all interesting.

One clown had a bulldog that was trained to do tricks. He walked on his two front feet and rolled over and over on command. His best trick was smoking the clown's pipe. The dog held the pipe between his teeth and puffed smoke from his mouth.

The clown was interacting continuously with the crowd beside the street. Because Norbert had ventured into the street wearing his colorful sailor suit, he was a prime target. The clown took the pipe from the bulldog's mouth and offered it to Norbert. The bulldog, obviously jealous of the attention the clown was giving Norbert, jumped high around Norbert and barked loudly. Norbert rapidly retreated to the sidewalk and the safety of the shade tree and his family.

Dark Shadows of Farm Life

Later in the summer and early fall, when the harvest was in full swing, the task of milking the cow in the morning was passed to Rosie. After breakfast she took a small pail of crushed corn with a small scoop of soybean meal to the field. She coaxed the cow away from the herd and through the wire gate with the pail of crushed corn. Knowing what to expect, the cow always came rapidly when Rosie called.

Then on one particular morning, the cow did not come when called. After several calls with no success, Rosie went into the field to investigate. The field itself included hills and ravines that were invisible from several angles. Had the herd escaped the field and strayed onto a neighbor's farm?

To Rosie's surprise she found the herd inside the field, but as she walked farther over the hill, she saw the milk cow lying in an awkward position beside the fence. When she got closer, she could see that the cow was dead. The large-framed yellow Guernsey cow had a wire from a bale of hay tied around her neck. The other end of the wire was tied to a fence post. It was obvious that as the cow pulled backward and the wire loop tightened, she had pulled hard enough to hang herself. The question was: how did this happen?

Rosie quickly went to the field where the men were working. They immediately went to investigate the mishap. It was obvious that this could not have happened accidently. Some person had to be involved.

The first likely suspect was Little Joe Langley who lived alone in a dilapidated house near Clifty Creek. Most of his house had collapsed, leaving only one room that was protected from the weather. Little Joe had no obvious way to provide for himself. Would he have tied the cow to the post to milk her?

Little Joe, a middle-aged man, had lived alone as a recluse in the abandoned house since his mother died. He was severely autistic, a condition defined in that day as "odd." As he grew up, his father put strong pressure on him to "act normal." When he was a young teenager, able to handle a gun, he had shot and killed his father. He was released to the custody of his mother because of his questionable mental condition.

After his mother died, Little Joe had rejected help from relatives and friends and had isolated himself in the old dilapidated house. Neighbors said that Little Joe lived off the land. He fished, gathered wild nuts and berries and trapped squirrels, chipmunks and birds. One neighbor said that he had seen a mole skin, evidence that Little Joe had eaten ground-moles.

Joe Esker and Paul went to see Little Joe. They asked him about the cow, but he denied any involvement. They tried to convince him that if he was hungry, he could ask and they would provide food. They offered to employ him in the harvest and pay him for his work. All offers were refused.

The dead cow was dragged by the workhorses to the farthest corner of the field, where it was eaten by the buzzards, foxes, opossums, and stray dogs.

One day Norbert mustered the courage to investigate the rotting carcass and the many buzzards. He surprised a large opossum eating in the stomach cavity of the cow. The opossum was reluctant to leave even after Norbert yelled at him.

The story was *not* told throughout the community. If the law had gotten involved, Little Joe could have been sent to an insane asylum. His mother, who had been designated as his guardian when Joe killed his father, had protected him from prison and the asylum. No supportive psychiatric programs existed at that time.

Later in the fall, Little Joe came to the house. Instead of knocking at the door, he waited out of sight until Joe Esker and Paul left the house after lunch. He approached them as they went to the barn and asked for kitchen matches. While Paul talked to Little Joe, Joe Esker returned to the house and grabbed a handful of matches from the tin match box on the wall. He stuffed them into a paper bag already holding the left-over cornbread and fried chicken from lunch. So Little Joe got not only matches but some food.

The Mail Carrier

The mailboxes for the rural delivery of mail were about a mile from the farm on Salt River Road. The mailman, John McDonald, left the Leitchfield post office and followed the dirt roads. When he got to St. Paul Road, he traveled west to the Salt River Road that led back to Leitchfield.

Mr. McDonald rode a large draft horse. The horse was a dark bay color with a black mane, tail and fetlocks. At times, the quantity of mail was so great with packages from the Sears Roebuck Catalog that the saddle bags and packages hung from the four corners of the saddle. Because the weather, the mud roads and the quantity of mail were constantly changing, the timing of Mr. McDonald's arrival at the mailboxes was erratic.

There were some half-dozen mailboxes at the corner of Salt River Road, belonging to the farm families who lived farther away from the main road. The farmers' wives with their children who were not in school would sometimes meet and wait for the mailman. This provided a social time for the women isolated on the remote farms. Rosie usually depended on Paul or Joe Esker to get the mail. But when a package was expected from Sears Roebuck, Rosie would wait for the mailman. This sometimes required walking to the mailbox two or three consecutive days until the package arrived.

Mr. McDonald delivered the mail on horseback until Jeeps became available after WWII. He then bought a four-wheel-drive Jeep to travel the mud roads. Unfortunately, the loud noise of the jeep could drown out the noise of an approaching train, and one day Mr. McDonald was killed in a collision with the train when it crossed the road at the edge of Leitchfield.

Borrowed Sugar

Late in the summer, as the apples in the small orchard ripened, Rosie planned one day to make an apple cobbler for lunch. After peeling and cooking the apples, she realized that she did not have enough sugar to complete the recipe. Rosie, and especially Norbert, was extremely disappointed.

They started planning ways to solve the problem. Since the store was two miles away, that option was disregarded. The next option was to borrow sugar from a neighbor, of whom the nearest were the Langleys who lived a half mile away. They would likely have sugar or sorghum molasses to sweeten the cobbler.

Norbert begged to be allowed to walk to the Langley's house to borrow sugar, although he had never walked the footpath through the woods alone. He knew the direction, but he had always been with his mother and father when they visited the Langleys. After persistent begging, Norbert was allowed to go. He would leave at 10:45, and arrive about 11:00, play with Jay and Anna for one-half hour, and arrive home at 11:45. Rosie would have time to finish the cobbler for lunch.

After Norbert got out of sight of the house and barn, and started over the hill through the woods, the surroundings were less familiar. Other foot-paths, used by fishermen and hunters, branched off the main path. Was he on the correct path? Then, when he heard a rooster crow in the direction he was going, his confidence was renewed.

By the time Norbert had played a half-hour with the Langley children, his interpretation of the instructions had changed. The "half-hour of play" instruction had been revised to "hour and a half".

Bessie, the mother, could not convince Norbert otherwise, so Norbert sat on the porch while the Langleys ate lunch, waiting for the children to come out to play some more. He arrived home at 12:45 p.m. instead of 11:45 a.m., as his mother had planned, so she was glad to see him.

Little Brother Samuel

Samuel, born the previous November in the Whitfill cabin, had progressed rapidly. He could walk when he was only eight months old. Rosie explained the fast progress by commenting that the floor of the cabin was so rough that it made his knees sore when he crawled. To prevent the soreness, he skipped the crawling stage and started walking early.

One evening when Rosie and Norbert were shelling corn for the chickens, Samuel was playing outside the chicken lot. They watched him start walking down the dirt path toward the barn. He was almost ten months old. They followed him, amazed at his ability to walk such a distance without falling. When Samuel got to the driveway of the barn he hesitated only a moment before spotting the stairs that led to the hayloft. He started to climb, reaching the height even with Rosie's shoulders before she rescued him.

Rosie and Norbert bragged about Samuel's athleticism, joking with relatives that Samuel would soon be throwing down fodder for the milk cow. Samuel liked to go to the barn. He could peep through the cracks and watch the pig and the calf. At other times, as Rosie was milking the cow, the horses would extend their heads into the driveway to investigate the small intruder. These were real live creatures that Rosie read about in the nursery books.

The next summer, after the family moved to Joe Esker's home farm, this curiosity about the barn would get Samuel into trouble. After supper, Paul usually returned to the barn to turn the horses into the pasture for the night. They could eat the green grass and enjoy the cool night breezes. In the barn which was much warmer, they would have been eating dry hay or corn fodder from the previous fall.

Norbert and Samuel were playing in the fenced yard under the silver poplar shade trees where Paul had hung a rope swing. Rosie called Norbert inside to give him a pail of scraps, left from preparing dinner, for the pigs. Norbert carried the pail to the barn where Paul instructed him to pour the scraps into the pigs' trough. Both horses with bridles stood in the driveway ready to be led to the pasture. Paul was busy tightening a shoe on Prince's hoof. When Norbert returned to the barn, hoping that he might ride one of the horses the short distance to the pasture, he saw Samuel squeezing through the barn doors at the other end of the driveway. Samuel had also squeezed through two gates on the way to the barn.

Samuel carried a stick that he had picked up on the way. He walked close to Dock's leg and hit him with the stick. The surprised, gentle horse reacted by kicking in the direction of Samuel. Samuel fell to the ground and screamed. Blood immediately covered his face. Paul grabbed him in his arms and ran to the pond to wash the blood away to see how badly he was cut. Samuel responded, "Don't throw me in the pond!" So Paul knew that, although the injury was serious, Samuel was fully conscious.

Paul carried Samuel to the house where he and Rosie wrapped bandages around the boy's head to slow the bleeding. The decision was made to rush Samuel to the doctor. The closest neighbor who owned a car was Rosie's Uncle Jim Douglas Milliner who lived about a mile away. Paul, carrying Samuel, jumped on one of the horses and galloped away toward Jim Douglas' farm. He hoped that Jim would drive him to Dr. Phelps's office which was eight or ten miles away in Leitchfield.

A few hours after dark Paul and Samuel returned. Samuel's face, except one eye and a corner of his mouth, was covered with bandages. The sharp iron shoe on the hoof of the horse had cut a semicircle gash from the center of Samuel's forehead to his chin. Neither his eyes nor his few teeth were damaged, but for the next week, until he returned to the doctor, he could only eat liquid foods through a straw. He drank milk and ate soups followed by Orange Crush soft drinks that Paul bought for a desert. Samuel recovered rapidly with minor scars that disappeared as he grew with time.

A Trip to the Mill

During most weeks, a trip to the mill was needed. The young chicks needed cracked corn. The milk cow or a heifer with a first calf needed crushed corn. Cornmeal was needed in the kitchen and high protein supplements were needed for the laying hens and the milk cow. Many times this trip was scheduled for Saturday afternoon after the week's work was completed and Norbert usually accompanied Paul on this trip.

On Saturday afternoon, Drake's store and mill were busy, so Paul might have to get in line and wait for his turn at the mill. At this local meeting place, unmarried men and women, some who had worked as far away as Louisville, gathered for the afternoon. Someone might have bought a new car and brought it to the store to show it to their friends.

The country store at the corner of the St. Paul and the Salt River Roads had been established as a company store many years before when tar and black rock had been mined nearby in Black Rock Holler. The miners had been paid with a company currency which they could only spend at the company store. Now the mine was closed and the store was no longer a company store.

When automobiles became popular, the state roads were converted from gravel roads to asphalt and a narrow-track railroad had been extended from Big Clifty west to the mines. The corner was still popular in the Tar Hill community and Saturday afternoon was the busiest time of the week. Usually a crap game or card game was going on in the shade of the store. Several men who worked away from home in the counties where whiskey was sold carried bottles in their pockets. The illegal moonshine whiskey was hidden a safe distance from the store in case the County Sheriff stopped by.

Paul knew everyone. He had played fiddle music for the square dances held in many homes nearby. Someone might invite him inside the mill out of sight and offer him a drink of whiskey from their bottle. Paul would take a sip from the bottle after he had looked at the label to see what he was drinking. Or, one of the men might whisper in Paul's ear, "There is a jug of moonshine under that sassafras bush down the road. Stop as you go home and get a drink." As he drove home, passing the sassafras bush, he might comment, "There is the sassafras bush; see the jug? I hope no one sees it."

About this time, Norbert was anticipating opening the small brown paper bag to sample the candy orange slices or the chocolate drops that they had bought from the glass cabinet in the store. Most of the candy would be shared with the whole family when they returned home.

Neighbors Helping Neighbors

If Paul and Norbert had turned north on Salt River Road, the first house they passed was that of Hosscat Burkhead. His real name was Else Burkhead. Hosscat's wife had died of tuberculosis just a few years before, leaving him with thirteen children to support.

Hosscat was a jack-of-all-trades. He cut hair as a self-trained barber for the men of the neighborhood, 25cents a cut. He sharpened tools either with a file or with a grindstone powered with a hand crank. The customer might have to supply the hand-power if Hosscat's children were in school. He had a simple blacksmith shop with a firebox that burned coal, and a bellows to increase the heat required to shape iron. He could repair shoes if the soles had come loose or if the seams needed a rivet in the leather.

Most of the farmers of the neighborhood regarded Hosscat's situation with much sympathy, so they gave him all their business in his fields of expertise. Paul and Joe Esker went there for their haircuts. Before the farm work started in the spring, they took the axes, the hoes and the plow points to be sharpened. The hoes and the plow points, working in the rough, rocky soil, usually needed heating and extending on the anvil before they were sharpened and tempered.

Hosscat also had a reputation around the community of Tar Hill as a hunter. He owned three hounds that he hunted with to tree opossums, raccoons and squirrels. He ate the wild game and sold the furs. Neighbors said that he ate the young crows that he collected from the crow's nests before they were old enough to fly, helping the farmers by thinning the crow population. Crows were especially adept at pulling the first emerging corn sprouts from the ground. They ate the seed corn kernel.

Walking two or three miles to hunt the squirrels that congregated in the woods bordering the corn fields was Hosscat's habit. Most of the farmers appreciated the fact that Hosscat controlled the scavengers, but others regarded him as a trespasser. When confronted by one of these farmers, Hosscat explained that he had saved several bushels of corn for the farmer by killing the squirrels. The farmer responded, "It's a damn poor farmer who cannot feed a few squirrels!"

Hosscat's hunting resulted in his death. Once, when he and his son were hunting groundhogs in a thick stand of corn, his son accidently shot and killed him.

Goodby Joe Esker

Joe Esker sold his farms in the fall of 1940. The hogs and the cattle were sold at the Bourbon Stockyard in Louisville. The horses and some of the farm equipment were sold to local farmers. They all knew that any trade with Joe Esker was honest and reliable. Paul bought a few pieces of small farm equipment: the single and double shovel plows and a one-row harrow. He also bought an old A-harrow that he would rebuild a few years later, replacing the wooden frame and taking the iron spikes to the blacksmith to reshape and sharpen. The remaining farm and household items were sold at a farm auction.

The corn tops, then bundled fodder still in the field, were moved to an adjoining farm as winter feed for Paul's few animals.

When everything had been sold and Joe Esker's moving date was set, the neighbors gathered at Joe Esker's house for a final farewell. He would be moving out of state to a new job in Indianapolis, Indiana, a job he had gotten through his political connections. Since he had few close relatives in Kentucky, he probably would not visit often.

All of the neighbors gathered: the Langleys, the Milliners, the Whitfills, the Johnsons, the Conders, the Lucases, and the Hazlewoods. All of the women brought food already prepared: potato salad, fried chicken, bowls of vegetables, Kool-Aid, radishes and lettuce, pies and cakes—the best of everything. The kitchen tables were moved into the yard under the silver poplar shade trees. Sawhorses were arranged to support platforms of rough lumber. Spare tablecloths and bed sheets covered the tables.

Everyone ate their fill. After dinner, they started a ball game in the lot between the house and the barn. Someone decided that they should have watermelons before they went home, but the watermelons and cantaloupes on the farm were finished. Willie Langley knew that Denny Board, south of Clifty Creek, grew Klickley Sweet melons, a long-season melon that was currently ripening.

While the crowd played ball, Paul and Willie rode the workhorses for a fast trip to the Boards to buy melons. They returned about an hour later with four large Klickley Sweet watermelons that were fully ripe, dark red, sweet and tasty. The ball game ended immediately when Paul and Willie arrived.

Everyone enjoyed the tasty watermelons and said their goodbyes to Joe Esker. Many of these neighbors would not see Joe Esker again, since he lived and worked for about 20 years in Indianapolis. He visited periodically to see his sister, his nephew and his niece. During these visits, he usually also visited Rosie and Paul.

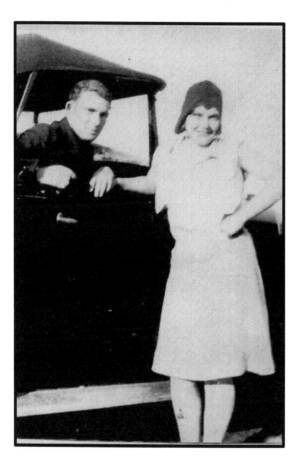

Paul and Rosie Clark
on their wedding day
1932

Above: 1940 Rosie and Paul Clark
with Norbert on the Condor Farm

Below: Norbert in his sailor suit, with Spot
Photo taken by a neighborhood salesgirl

Sara Marie and Jean Milliner (in back);
Sammy and Norbert Clark (front)
At Lizzie Whitfill's house 1941

A cabin similar to the Whitfill cabin

The Milliner family, from back left: Gilbert, Ace, John Riley, Jim
Martin, Mary Alta, Charles A.   Front: Lydia Ann, Marcella/Marty
or little Grandma, and Josephine

Left: Ike as a young man
Right: Ike and Janie Clark 1930

Above: Ike in more prosperous times

Paul's fiddlle on Great Grandma Marty's quilt

**Above: A young Mary Alta and Edward Milliner, Rosie's parents
Below: Later in life: Mary Alta and Edward Milliner**

Chimney rocks from the log cabin where
Rosie and Norbert was born.

Tood's Ford, where three roads converged
to cross the shallow water

**Meeting Creek, where Paul slipped from the
foot-log on his way to church.**

**Dirt road on old Langley farm, eroded deeply.
The original road would have been without tree leaves.**

Today's version of the Milliner farm

where Rosie was born

Edward Milliner's parents

Paul and Rosie's children
Front, left to right: Anna Jean, Kathleen, Martina, Christine
Back, left to right: Norbert, Samuel, Daniel, Lowell

FOLLOWING PAGES: MAP DRAWN BY Norbert Clark showing the farms on which Paul and Rosie Clark lived.

Maps showing locations of the Clark farms

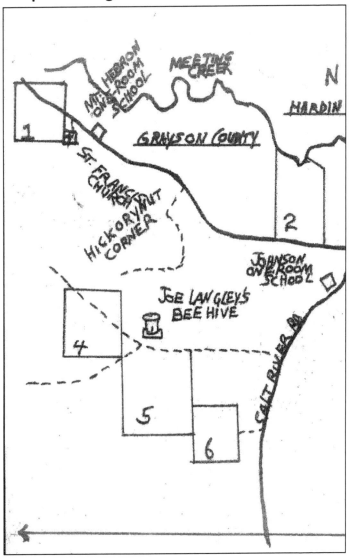

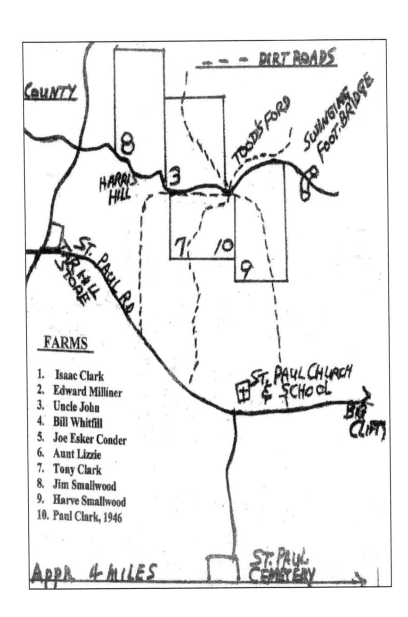

COUNTY

— — — DIRT ROADS

TOOD'S FORD

SWINGING FOOT-BRIDGE

8

HARRIS HILL

3

ST. PAUL RD
TAR HILL STORE

7   10

9

FARMS

1. Isaac Clark
2. Edward Milliner
3. Uncle John
4. Bill Whitfill
5. Joe Esker Conder
6. Aunt Lizzie
7. Tony Clark
8. Jim Smallwood
9. Harve Smallwood
10. Paul Clark, 1946

ST. PAUL CHURCH & SCHOOL

BIG CLIFTY

APPR. 4 MILES

ST. PAUL CEMETERY

107

Details about Farms

(Corresponding to Numbers on Map)

1. The farm of Isaac and Janie Clark, Paul's parents. Paul was taken out of the one-room Mt. Hebron School when in the sixth grade to help support the family. He worked there until he married Rosie in 1932.

2. The farm of Edward and Mary Alta Milliner. Rosie was born there in a log cabin built by her Milliner ancestors. Rosie and Paul also lived there in the original log cabin for four years after they were married. Rosie experienced two stillbirths and then Norbert's birth in 1936 in this old log cabin.

3. The farm of Uncle John and Aunt Dora Langley. Paul and Rosie rented the large, rough hill farm as sharecroppers after the furniture factory in which Paul worked in Louisville was destroyed by the flood of 1937. They moved into an abandoned cabin on the farm. Uncle John sold the farm one year later and Rosie and Paul moved.

4. The farm originally owned by Bill Whitfill and sold to Joe Esker Conder. Paul and Rosie rented the farm as sharecroppers and reclaimed and moved into an abandoned log cabin. Their second son, Samuel, was born there.

5. Joe Esker Conder's home farm. After a year living in the Whitfill log cabin, Joe Esker asked Rosie and Paul to move into his more modern farm house. As sharecroppers they

worked and shared in the produce from both of Joe Esker's farms until he sold the farms in the fall of 1940.

6. The farm of Aunt Lizzie Whitfill, an elderly unmarried lady. The once productive farm had not been cultivated for several years during the depression. As a share cropper, Paul cleared the land and rebuilt the fences until Aunt Lizzie decided to sell the farm in the fall of 1942. Paul and Rosie's first daughter, Martina, was born there.

7. This farm was owned by Paul's first cousin, Tony Clark. The dog-trot log house and the log barn had been built by Paul's grandfather, Charles Langley, in 1880. The extremely hilly farm was eroded and unproductive. As sharecroppers, Paul and Rosie struggled on the farm until Tony was forced to return to the farm and they moved again.

8. A large, rough hill-farm owned by the Smallwoods for several generations. It provided a tremendous improvement for the sharecroppers over the previous Tony Clark farm. The major disadvantage was its remote location on hilly dirt roads. It was far from school, church, feed mill and store. Daniel, the fourth child, was born there in 1944.

9. The Harve Smallwood farm was a sharecropper's dream. The farm house was comfortable and the land was productive with the exception of the abandoned field that Paul was asked to reclaim. The school and church were conveniently located on good roads. During this year Paul and Rosie, after struggling for fourteen years, were able to establish the financial foundation to buy their own place.

10. Paul and Rosie finally gained a toe-hold when they purchased the old Langley farm. They would not have to move again. However, because of the low productivity of the eroded rough hill-farm, Paul continued to rent adjacent land as a sharecropper. Lowell, 1946, Christina, 1948, Kathleen, 1950 and Anna Jean, 1952, were all born here.

9

Living with Aunt Lizzie

Paul and his family moved again while winding down the harvest at Joe Esker's farms. This time, it was a slow, gradual move to an adjacent farm owned by an elderly lady, Aunt Lizzie Whitfill. She was the sister of Bill Whitfill who had originally owned the hillside farm and the log cabin where Paul and Rosie lived after leaving Uncle John's farm in Hardin County.

Aunt Lizzie's house was not as spacious as Joe Esker's had been. There were three smaller rooms in an L-shape and an open porch. Aunt Lizzie moved into one room. Her only requirements were "A bed, a rocking chair, and a cook stove." Paul and Rosie could use the remainder of the house, the barn and the outbuildings like the smokehouse and the chicken house. They would miss the large screened porches and the convenience of the well-water outside the kitchen door. They would need to place wooden gutters under the eaves to catch water for washing, and they would need to carry clean water for drinking and cooking from a spring at the bottom of a steep hill in the holler.

Using rope halters, Paul led the milk cow and the heifer, born 18 months before on the Bill Whitfill farm. The heifer, half Jersey, would have a calf the following spring. The brood sow that had been saved from slaughter as a pig a year before was driven across the field with a rope tied to her hind leg. The pigs being raised for slaughter followed the sow. At Joe Esker's auction, Paul had bought the chicken box that was used to take chickens to market. Laying hens were transferred in the box as part of several small loads of household and farm items.

The short-distance move continued for a few weeks until the corn and the fodder were moved. This was Paul's share of the farm produce arranged by the contract with Joe Esker.

Good Neighbors

Aunt Lizzie's house was within a quarter mile of two other families. Willie Langley's family lived at the bottom of the hill to the south near Clifty Creek. Although he owned his farm, he was a subsistence farmer like Paul. Bill Whitfill's family lived across the holler to the east. Aunt Lizzie's house was also within sight of the Salt River Road, the main road from the Tar Hill community to the County Seat at Leitchfield. Mr. McDonald, the mailman on his horse, could be seen stuffing mail into the mailboxes posted on the side of the road.

The path to Bill Whitfill's house was so steep in places that steps were dug into the hill. Wooden stairs had been built to climb one steep rock ledge. Both Whitfill families had originally carried water from the spring in the holler. Bill had dug a well at his house but Aunt Lizzie still carried water from the spring. Paul, Rosie and Norbert would make many trips into the holler to carry cold, fresh spring water for drinking and cooking.

During the first winter, Rosie and Paul became more connected to the Bill Whitfill family. In the spring, they traded garden seeds and eggs from different breeds of chickens for hatching. When one of the Whitfill boys shot three ducks that were swimming on their farm pond, they shared one duck with Rosie and Paul.

Bill's wife, Florence, was Paul's cousin and her father, Leo Clark, was Paul's great-uncle. He lived with the Whitfill Family. Uncle Leo was in his 90s and was partially blind.

Leo was very social. He enjoyed playing cards or sharing a drink of the local whiskey. Because he was partially blind, someone usually sat with him helping him identify his cards and arranging them in his hand. Once identified and arranged, he could play the hand. Every card played by the other players was identified so that Leo could keep account of the game.

The game of pitch that they played was simple. Bidding identified a trump suit. The players were usually arranged in teams increasing the social aspect of the game.

Uncle Leo's hands would shake uncontrollably, but after drinking a whiskey toddy, his hands were calm and steady. A bottle of moonshine whiskey kept in the kitchen cupboard was always available as a medicinal drink.

Paul carried the kerosene lantern for the trip home because, after dark, the steep hills on the path were impassible without a light. Paul sometimes stopped on the way home to check a box trap or a snare set to catch a rabbit or a quail in the thickets near the path.

Another Abandoned Farm

Aunt Lizzie's farm had not been cultivated or pastured for several years, so Paul had to repair fences and gates. Two fields were selected to grow corn and hay. Late in the winter when weather permitted, he burned the broom sage and the wild grass that quickly established itself in all uncultivated fields. After burning the grass, he dug out the bushes and the briars before plowing the fields.

Paul planted the smaller fields with Korean clover. He and his cousin, Bennie Johnson, had bought a new McCormick-Deering mowing machine and a rake the previous year. They both planned to grow legumes as hay, an improvement over the corn fodder. The larger field would be plowed and planted with corn.

Because the thick stands of wild grass were evidence that the soil was extremely acid, Paul looked into a government program that promoted the use of agricultural lime to reduce the acidity of the soil. Aunt Lizzie agreed with the idea, so Paul ordered several truck-loads of lime that was delivered by large dump trucks and dumped into several piles around the fields.

Paul scattered the lime with a machine that converted Aunt Lizzie's farm wagon into a lime spreader. A sprocket was bolted onto one of the rear wheels of the wagon. A long, square–linked chain connected the drive sprocket to the gears of the spreader which was fastened to the rear end of the wagon bed. The feed-gate of the spreader was adjusted to deliver the correct tons-per-acre. First, the lime was shoveled from the pile on the ground into the wagon bed, from where it was shoveled continuously into the hopper of the spreader. The horses pulled the wagon forward at a fast walk. The rapidly revolving propeller at the bottom of the spreader threw the lime in a fan-shaped pattern about ten feet on each side of the wagon.

It soon became obvious that Paul was going to be kept busy shoveling the lime into the hopper, so he gave the driving lines to Norbert who was instructed to keep the team walking at a fast clip following an imaginary line parallel to the previous tracks. He was told to turn the team and wagon several steps before the end of the field so that the lime was not wasted in the fence row.

Norbert, age five, had only driven the horses in strictly controlled situations such as on the road home from the mill. If the gentle horses attempted to make a premature turn into the wrong road, Paul was there to take control.

Now, Norbert was alone in the front of the wagon. Paul was busy shoveling lime into the hopper, his back turned to the horses. If the horses slowed, he would tell Norbert to increase the speed. Norbert nervously tried to talk to the horses. "Gid up Dock! Gid up Prince!" He tried kicking the end gate of the wagon to scare the horses. Nothing worked until he used the leather check reins dangling around his feet to tap the horses on their rumps as he had seen Paul do.

Paul saw the problem and cut and trimmed a tall bush from the fence row. With that long switch, Norbert did not have to lean so far over the front of the wagon, but he had to learn how to use this switch. The first time he used it, the horses broke into a trot. He quickly learned to control the speed and the direction, dodging rocks and stumps. He learned to turn at the end without wasting lime in the fence rows and could guide the team and the wagon into the most convenient position for Paul to shovel the lime into the wagon. His skills and confidence grew rapidly as they spread the lime over both fields.

Norbert's newly gained skills would be used several times that spring. He would ride the drag to level the plowed field or use the large A-harrow, driving the horses while Paul attended to other chores like setting fence posts. Several times the harrow collected so many roots that its spikes did not scratch the ground. Norbert could not lift the harrow to remove the roots, so Paul was called to solve the problem, and then the work continued. In that summer when he turned five years old, Norbert was contributing to the progress of the family.

Aunt Lizzie's House Fire

Early in the spring when the daffodils were blooming, Rosie decided to build a fire near the woodpile to heat wash water. She needed extra hot water to wash the winter quilts. Norbert was riding his Christmas tricycle on the dirt paths that led to the chicken house, the woodpile and the barn. As he approached he saw smoke around the fieldstones that were the foundation of the house. When he told Rosie, she investigated and concluded that the wind had carried the smoke from the fire under the wash tub to the house. On Norbert's next trip down the path on his tricycle toward the house, he saw even more smoke, plainly coming from under the house.

This time, Rosie quickly ran into the house. Aunt Lizzie was sleeping on the bed while under the stove the fire had burned a hole through the floor. Without hesitating, Rosie ran to the woodpile and grabbed the heavy tub of wet quilts and wash water. She carried it into the house and dumped it upside down into the fire that had burned through the floor.

By now, Aunt Lizzie was awake, appearing somewhat groggy. Rosie instructed Norbert to run to the field to get Paul to help in case the fire was still burning under the floor.

Paul was plowing in the field farthest from the house. Norbert was not sure where he would find his father, but he ran as fast as he could in that direction. Paul saw Norbert running toward him yelling, "The house is on fire!" Without another word, Paul unhitched Dock and with the trace chains still dangling leaped on the horse and rode at its fastest gallop toward the house. No doubt he was remembering the house fire when he was twelve years old, when his family lost everything, and escaped in the night with only their night-clothes.

Norbert was left with Prince who was upset by the loud yelling and the activity around him. His mate was gone! Norbert was unable to control the nervous horse and Prince turned toward the house dragging the plow on its side across the plowed ground. Norbert could not run fast enough to catch the horse, but Prince soon tired from that heavy pulling and Norbert was able to unhitch him and lead him to the house.

When Norbert got to the house, everyone was relaxed, smiling and talking about how lucky they had been. Aunt Lizzie had moved her rocking chair to the porch into the fresh air. The fire had been completely quenched by the tub of quilts and water. Paul had removed several of the rocks that underpinned the house so he could see under the house in two directions. No embers had escaped Rosie's deluge of wet quilts and wash water.

The cause of the fire was simple. Although there was plenty of wood on the woodpile, Aunt Lizzie had attempted to burn dead limbs that had fallen from the trees during the winter. She could not break some of the limbs to a length that would allow her to close the door of the stove. After collecting and breaking the limbs, Aunt Lizzie had laid down on the bed to rest. As she slept, the long sticks of wood had partially burned leaving the long sticks, still burning, to fall to the floor. In a more air-tight house, she might have suffocated.

The Spring Tornado

A few days after the scare with the house fire, a tall dark cloud appeared in the southwestern sky. The afternoon was warm and the sun was shining at the farm. The high, dark green clouds rapidly rolled across the sky. Suddenly, as the clouds moved closer, the sun disappeared; the temperature dropped and the hail began to fall. On the galvanized steel roof of the house, the noise was deafening. Ice balls, some as large as hen eggs, covered the yard.

Then, almost as rapidly as it had appeared in the southwest, the storm disappeared in the southeast. Paul picked up enough of the large hail to fill a ten quart pail for ice water.

117

The next day, he heard from the mailman that a strong tornado had destroyed many buildings a few miles south of the farm. Paul's uncle Jim Henry Clark lived on a farm in the direct path of the storm. All the buildings on his farm near Big Clifty had been destroyed. His wife, cushioned in some of the quilts and bed clothes, had been blown a distance from the farm house, but had survived. Several acres of timber that Jim Henry had protected for firewood and lumber around the farm had been reduced to splinters.

The Lizzie Whitfill farm had escaped another catastrophe.

Farm Routines

The two year old half-Jersey heifer delivered her calf late in the spring. In the heifer, the nervous characteristics attributed to the Jersey breed were evident to the extreme. When the calf was born, the heifer refused to let anyone into her stall. Paul cut holes in the walls on opposite sides of the stall and pushed several long poles through to pin her against the wall. This was the typical procedure night and morning for a couple of weeks until she would stand for milking. She produced a good veal calf and a good quantity of rich, creamy milk that eventually doubled the income from cream.

Paul had raised a plentiful corn crop the previous year on Joe Esker's farm. This allowed the number of chicks raised and sold as fryers to be increased to two hundred. The sow also had a litter of eight pigs, six of which were fattened and sold at market weight. Two of the pigs were saved for meat and lard for the family.

Paul traded work almost weekly with the Johnsons who lived on the south side of Clifty Creek. Mrs. Cora Johnson was Paul's cousin. The Boards, Denny and Lettie, who owned a large farm near the

Johnson's farm, needed help during the busy seasons. Paul sometimes traded work but was often paid for his labor.

Lettie was a good musician. She always asked Paul to bring his fiddle when he came to work on their farm. After lunch, when time allowed, they would play the fiddle, the guitar and the piano while they rested from the farmwork.

The summer and the fall continued without much more excitement. Trading work with the Whitfills, the Johnsons, the Langleys and the Boards, the corn was topped for fodder. The hay was cut and stacked in three tall stacks outside the barnyard fence. The tobacco was cut and stored for drying.

During the first week of December, for no apparent reason, Samuel and Norbert were moved to a pallet on the floor in Aunt Lizzie's room. Grandma Clark visited and stayed overnight. The next morning Rosie was still in bed, but with a new baby. A baby sister, named Martina Rose, had been born, a big surprise to the other children. Aunt Frances, as she had done when Samuel was born, was again asked to stay the ten days that Rosie was required to stay in bed. Grandma Clark, who had been the midwife, immediately returned to Mount Hebron to be with her invalid husband, Ike.

Mysterious Conversations

Many neighbors visited over the next few days while Rosie was in bed. They were all talking about "the war" and the possibilities that men would be called into the army. Martina had been born on December 5, 1941, just before the bombing of Pearl Harbor by the Japanese.

In the evening, Norbert and Paul visited the Whitfills, who owned a battery radio, to listen to the news. Norbert did not understand why the adults sat silently listening to the radio, since such a quiet atmosphere was unusual. On other visits, they might have listened to the Amos and Andy show. They'd have joked among themselves, laughing both at the radio programs and at their own jokes. At other times, they turned the radio off and visited, discussing their progress on the farm or the number of new pigs in a new litter.

Norbert sat close to Paul on the floor and listened quietly, trying to understand the problem. When the news ended, they turned the radio off and talked about the men who had been working in the field a few weeks before. Would they be there to burn the plant beds and plow the fields in the spring? Where would they go? How long would they be gone? Would they return home?

The trip home through the holler with the lantern was a silent one. Norbert's questions to Paul were answered with short explanations that he did not understand. The typical light-hearted conversations about the calls of the whippoorwills or the screech owls, or the bark of a distant fox, didn't happen.

Norbert would lie in bed thinking about the mysterious topics of conversation, the questions and the answers.

Hog Killing Time with Grandpa Edward

The weather was turning cold and Paul was planning to kill the two hogs. He guessed that they would weigh more than 300 pounds each, so he bought an extra 50-pound bag of salt at Drake's store. The Whitfills had a fifty gallon drum that he could borrow to heat the water to scald the hogs. He sharpened the butcher knives and cleaned the stone crocks for pickling the fatback. He built a shelf in the smokehouse where he would pack the hams, the shoulders and the bacon in salt.

The Whitfills had already killed their hogs. Paul had helped with the scalding, the gutting and cutting the sides of pork into hams, shoulders, bacon, etc. He'd been responsible for these jobs since he was a teenager at his home. The Whitfills gave him a pan of backbones and ribs, enough for a large pot of fresh pork. Later, they sent samples of their sausage, bragging about the perfect seasoning with red pepper and sage.

Rosie's father and mother came to help with the hog killing. Three of Rosie's younger sisters (Frances, Sarah Maria and Jean) also came to help and to care for the new baby.

Paul and Grandpa Edward made quick work of the slaughter. Grandpa Edward assured Paul that the hogs weighed even more than 300 pounds. By noon the hogs' carcasses were hanging on the pole, cleaned and cooling so that the cutting and trimming could proceed more precisely.

The hogs in the stall had been shot in the center of the brain. Immediately after they fell, the arteries in their throats were cut in order to pump the blood from the carcass. The carcass was loaded on the farm sled and pulled near the barrel of hot water. The water was hot enough to burn a finger, but it was not boiling. The barrel was tilted against the side of the sled at an angle. In this position, the carcass could more easily be pushed in and pulled out of the barrel by hand.

After the carcass was pushed into the hot water, it was rotated until the hair was loosened. Then it was reversed and the process was repeated on the other end of the hog. The loose hair was scraped off with scrapers and dull knives. The hairless carcasses were then hung with gambrel sticks between the hind legs and rinsed with clean water.

Paul and Grandpa Edward opened the hanging carcasses from the throat to the rear exposing the entrails and internal organs. Special caution was taken not to puncture the entrails whose smelly contents could contaminate the carcass. The green, bitter gall bladder attached to a leaf of the liver was removed as soon as the liver was exposed. Fresh liver was fried for lunch.

While the men were working with the hogs, the women were preparing for processing the meat. The sausage grinder that had been stored in the smokehouse was dismantled and cleaned. Empty glass jars were washed and sterilized in boiling water. The pots and pans for cooking the sausage and the organ meats were located for the next step of cooking and canning.

The black kettle was set up in the yard on the stones where the wash water was heated. It would be ready for rendering the fats into lard the next day. Paul would need to whittle a wooden paddle to stir the fat so that it would not burn at the bottom of the hot kettle. A burned taste in the lard would contaminate every dish to which it was added. Rosie and Granny also prepared a delicious dinner in celebration of the special event, the hog killing.

After lunch, the carcasses were split down the middle of the back bones with an ax. Each side was laid on the table of boards on the sawhorses. Paul and Grandpa were both experienced at breaking down the sides of pork. After the ribs and the loins were removed, the hams and the shoulders were separated from the midsection. The midsection was separated into bacon, fat back and fat trimmings for lard. The hams and shoulders were trimmed closely and the legs were cut off shortly above the knees.

Before the end of the day, the hams, the shoulders and the side and jowl bacon were packed in salt on the shelf in the smoke house.

Nothing was wasted. The fat was carefully stripped from the intestines. It was added to the belly fat and rendered into lard in a black iron kettle on a fire in the yard. All the skins that were removed in the process were rendered of fats in the kitchen oven and turned into lard and cracklings. The brittle pigskin cracklings could be salted and eaten as a snack or crushed and added to cornbread to add a unique taste of browned pork skin.

The lean trimmings from the hams and the shoulders, the back bones and the ribs were saved for sausage. The lean ends of the loins were also added to fat trimmings to be ground into sausage. The center pork chops from the loins were canned for a supply of meat the following summer. The trimmings, fat and lean, were seasoned with sage and red pepper grown in the garden the previous summer.

The sausage grinder was clamped to the center of a long board suspended between two chairs. A person sat on each end of the board. One person fed the meat into the grinder while the other person turned the handle. Paul had sharpened the blades of the grinder before starting the turning. The two persons on the board exchanged ends often to share the work. After aging until the next day to allow the sage and pepper tastes to saturate the sausage, the meat was cooked and canned. The lard rendered from the fats in the sausage was sufficient to cover the cooked sausage in the can.

The hog's heads and the shanks were boiled in a pot until the gristles, the ligaments and the tendons were tender. All the skins and the meats on the ears, the snout and the tail were separated from the bones. The complete mixture was seasoned with spices, poured in a pan and cooled. This jelly-like mass formed a loaf that could be sliced and used for sandwiches. This was called 'souse'.

The organ meats were processed into a loaf resembling braunschweiger. The liver, the heart, the kidneys and the tongue with other minor organs were cooked until tender. They were ground and flavored with vinegar and spices and formed into a loaf. The loaves were stored in the cold smokehouse and used a few slices at a time for sandwiches or lunches.

The lungs were cooked and shared with the dog and the cat for several meals. The brains were fried and mixed with scrambled eggs for a once-a-year breakfast. Backbones and ribs were cut into small pieces with the ax on a flat chopping block. They were cooked in a large pot and served for several meals until all the meat had been eaten. The many bones provided a feast for the dog and the cat.

The meats packed in salt in the smokehouse were monitored for a few weeks, and salt was added when necessary. When they no longer absorbed salt, the loose salt was brushed off and the meat was hung from the rafters for smoking. A bonnet made of metal roofing was hung around the meat to trap the smoke. A wash tub half filled with ashes was placed under the bonnet. A small pan of hot coals from the stove was placed on the center of the ashes.

The intention was to produce smoke by continuously adding green hickory chips and small sticks of wood to produce smoke without flames. That wood was cut from small green hickory saplings that contained no heartwood. As the green wood slowly burned, the bed of coals was self perpetuating. If the live coals were covered with the ashes in late evening, they were still hot in the morning.

The fire was attended from early morning until late evening for about a week. The temperature did not need to be monitored because the small bed of coals was sufficient to raise the temperature in the bonnet only slightly.

The smoking process was complete when the meat was brown and the surface was dry and firm to the touch. The meat was hung in the smoke house suspended on wires from the rafters until it was needed.

Time Marches On

The next year, 1942, was less exciting than 1941. Because the crops the previous year had not been as productive as expected, Paul and Aunt Lizzie decided to grow hay and corn in the same fields. There was no more lime to spread, but the lime applied the previous spring might have dissolved more thoroughly and reduced the acidity of the soil. The result would be that the crops would absorb more nutrients and produce heavier yields.

The broom sage, the bushes and the briars had also been eliminated the spring before. Aunt Lizzie had learned not to burn wood that was too long for the cook stove, and the Jersey heifer that had caused trouble the previous spring had been trained.

Paul cut the bushes and saplings in the fence row leading out the lane to Salt River Road and the mailboxes and used the brush for burning a plant bed. He cut mulberry posts and built a barbed wire fence beside the lane. This permitted the convenience of opening another field for pasturing the two cows and horses.

Military Men

Five boys in the neighborhood who had helped with the farm work in previous years were talking about going into the U.S. Army. Rosie's brothers, Andy William and Sylvester Herbert, were eligible for the draft. Tommy Whitfill, Bill Whitfill's son, and Joe-Pat* and Bennie Johnson, three cousins of Paul, were all eligible. (*Joe-Pat was a typical Kentucky nomenclature.)

Paul himself received a letter from the draft board alerting him to register for the draft. He had been thirty years old in January and was considered too old for the draft at that time, but the draft age

125

increased throughout the war. Until the war ended, Paul constantly feared that he would be drafted.

The five neighbors and others from outside the community were in the army by fall. Parents of the boys in the closely-knit community invited the neighbors for a going away dinner for their sons, and tears were shed at these dinners. The war and the drafted boys were a main topic of conversation among all the neighbors.

After basic training was completed a few months later, the boys returned home for a furlough before being shipped over-seas. The families again got together to see the boys in their crisply pressed uniforms and their short haircuts. When compared to their farm-boy image, in patched denim overalls with straw hats and long hair, the boys were barely recognizable. They were shaking hands they had never shaken before and standing rigidly straight, addressing the men and women as "Sir" and "Mam". Their voices were clear and strong compared to their bashful, stammering voices of the past.

The trip home from these gatherings was usually in silence. Most of these boys would be gone for two or three years---some forever. Before the war ended in 1945, four boys from the parish of Saint Paul had been killed. Two Clarks and two Milliners, relatives of Paul and Rosie, had died. To honor their service, a monument with the names of these four boys was installed in front of St. Paul Church

School Days

Norbert was six years old in the spring of 1942, so he would soon be going to school. The one-room Johnson Public Elementary School was located about a mile away on Salt River Road. This was the same school that his mother, Rosie, had attended for eight years. Two of Rosie's younger sisters and one brother still attended the school.

The schedule of the school conformed to the labor needs of the farm families. Classes began in July after the busy labor demands of planting and cultivating the farm crops. It would adjourn again in September for a few weeks during the high labor demands of the harvest.

Several of the Johnsons, the Whitfills and the Langleys passed near Aunt Lizzie's house every day on their way to the Johnson school house. Rosie knew the school teacher and arranged to send Norbert to the school to introduce him to the discipline of the school room. Norbert would sit with his Aunt Jean who was in the second grade.

Norbert was up early dressing in his new school clothes. He helped his mother pack his lunch—a sausage patty on a biscuit from breakfast, an apple and a small jar of milk. His lunch pail was a four-pound lard pail. In his book satchel, which hung almost to his knees, he took a tablet of paper and a pencil that Paul had sharpened with his pocket knife. He walked to the mailbox early and waited for the neighborhood children. School was fun, especially the walk to and from school with the other students.

The school year at St. Paul's parochial school would begin in September. Transportation with a blue panel truck, 'The Blue Goose', was arranged, so several of the Catholic students in the one-room public school transferred to the parochial school three miles away on St. Paul road. Students still walked the mile on Salt River Road together; then, at the Tar Hill store, they caught the Blue Goose bus for the ride to St. Paul School.

The parochial school was a two-room school. With the introduction of the school bus, the number of new students in the first three grades increased to fill one of the rooms with thirty or forty students. This was an extraordinary responsibility for the young, first-year teacher, Sister Mary Estelle.

The sixth, seventh and eighth grades filled the second room. Because of the increased number of students, a third room was opened in the convent for the fourth and fifth grades. Another small room was built in which a ninth grade was started. After that, a grade was added each year until the high school was established..

In the mid-1940s, few of the students, like their parents, advanced beyond the eighth grade. This arrangement continued until the new high school was opened in the fall of 1946.

Ike's Death

On October 5, 1942, Paul's father, Ike, died. After the embalming, Ike's body was brought home. During the time that his body remained in the home, the neighbors held twenty-four hour vigil. One neighbor, Jimmy Miller, built a wooden box for the grave and delivered it to the house. The day before the funeral, Paul and his brother David harnessed the horses to take the box to the graveyard in the farm wagon. The cemetery was located about a quarter-mile up the hill from the house.

Then Uncle Jim Douglas Milliner arrived in his new red pickup truck and volunteered to take the box to the cemetery. Paul and David rode in the back of the truck to stabilize the box on the rough dirt road. Norbert, six years old, ran up the hill behind the truck to watch them lower the box into the grave. They used the leather driving lines from the horses' harness to lower the box into the ground.

After the funeral the next day, all the relatives and many of the neighbors returned the short distance down the hill to the farm house. The women were in the kitchen organizing the luncheon, most of which had been brought by those attending. Several of the pots contained chicken and dumplings, or end-of-the-season vegetables such as turnips, black-eyed peas or Kentucky Wonder green beans with many mature beans. Pans of fried chicken and blackberry cobblers were plentiful, but Grandma Janie was worried that there were not enough forks for everyone.

The men moved chairs to the yard under the red cedar trees at the south end of the house and laid boards from around the barn across blocks of wood for additional seating. One of the men stored a bottle of whiskey in the harness room in the barn. As the men went to the barn to 'go to the bathroom,' they could take a swig from the bottle.

Several small children ran unorganized among their fathers, uncles and cousins, slapping knees and kicking feet. Someone soon responded to the mayhem and asked a couple of the teenage girls to take control of the young children. The children responded enthusiastically playing drop-the-handkerchief, ring-around-the-roses and mother-may-I.

After the lunch, the crowd rapidly dispersed. Three of the Clark brothers, Bernard, Johnny and Lawrence, and their families who had travelled from Richmond, Indiana, were quickly on their way home. The neighbors said goodbye to these friends whom they had not seen for several years and hitched their teams for their journeys home. Paul and Rosie helped David, the youngest son, who with his young family lived with his parents. Together they put things in order.

10
THE OLD LANGLEY FARM

Moving the Easy Way

In the fall of 1942, Aunt Lizzie decided that she wanted to sell the farm. Since Paul and Rosie were not prepared to buy the farm, they would have to move again. The move was well organized. Rosie and Paul had moved six times in the last six years. Wavy Drake with his truck was hired to move the larger household items: the stoves, the beds, the kitchen table, the cupboard, the chairs and farm equipment. These items would have required several trips in the small farm wagon. As the family had grown and Paul had become more involved in farming, the quantity of household items and farm equipment had rapidly expanded.

Paul would haul his share of the crops as the harvest progressed. Aunt Lizzie's share would be stored in her barn and crib. The business arrangement for this unique situation, where the farm had not been cultivated for several years before Paul and his family arrived, required that Aunt Lizzie retain only one third of the crops. Paul, as the tenant, got two thirds. No money was involved but Paul had paid for the fertilizer and the seeds. Under this arrangement, Paul fed his crop to livestock to increase their value. Aunt Lizzie sold her share to pay taxes and provide for her livelihood.

Janie's Childhood Home

The farm to which they were moving was owned by Paul's first cousin, Tony Clark, and was located near St. Paul Church and school. Tony had gotten a job at the Reynolds Metal Company in Louisville and had moved his family there.

The buildings on the farm were old. The original log structures had been built by Paul's grandfather in 1880. The house, which had originally been built as a two room, dog-trot log cabin with two large fireplaces, had been overhauled. It was now a four room house with a back porch and two brick flues for a sheet metal stove and a cook stove. One of the stone chimneys was still standing at the south end of the house, but it was not used because of cracks in the mortar.

The original log barn and a separate crib with a small shed still existed. A small hen house, structurally questionable, and several unkempt apple and peach trees were present. The garden fence would need to be rebuilt. Water would be carried from a spring under a steep hill, similar to the situation on Aunt Lizzie's farm.

This was the farm where Paul's mother, Janie, had grown up. The house had been built when she was "old enough to carry a small pail of water from the spring to the workmen." Since then, the farm had changed ownership several times. The fields were rough and hilly and the topsoil had eroded in many places so that nothing grew on the bare knolls. The land's only advantage was that the farm was within a short distance to the school and church.

A New Red Farm Wagon

Paul had been using farm wagons owned by Joe Esker and Aunt Lizzie when he lived on their farms, so he now bought a new wagon.

Sam Terry who owned the hardware store in Big Clifty ordered the wagon from the Owensboro Wagon Company and it was shipped unassembled to Big Clifty by train.

Paul took the team to Big Clifty to bring the wagon home. With harnesses on the horses, he rode Dock and led Prince. At Big Clifty he assembled the wagon and brought it home, standing in the new wagon bed. Rosie and the children met Paul at the barn to admire the new red wagon. He would build sideboards for gathering corn from wide poplar boards found in the barn. Paul and Rosie would move three times with this wagon before they finally owned a farm.

Norbert's New Friend

On his one mile walk down the dirt road to meet the school bus, Norbert found a new friend. The first time he saw the tall, old white-haired man standing beside the road, he was inclined to run back home. But, as he hesitated, the man spoke quietly and extended a hand holding a shining red apple.

The man's name was Clint Nichols. He and his wife, Sarah, lived in a little house behind the orchard that extended almost to the road. They had no relatives in the community and, out of friendship, Mr. Nichols would meet Norbert every morning with an apple for as long as the apples lasted.

Mr. Nichols was a handyman who owned tools for repairing stringed musical instruments and clocks. Paul's fiddle, which had started to separate along the glue lines, was taken to Mr. Nichols for repair. In exchange, Paul would plow and cultivate Mr. Nichols' garden in the spring.

Tony Clark's old hilly farm, now their home, was similar to the Whitfill farm where they had lived four years before. Several gullies in the hilly fields were impassible. The thickets of bushes and briars would need to be dug or cut before the fields could be plowed. Paul collected the grubbing hoes and the ax and took them to Hosscat's blacksmith shop for sharpening in preparation for this project.

The most promising part of the farm was the few acres of highly productive bottom land under the hill along the south side of Meeting Creek. Paul would harvest more corn from this productive bottom land than he would realize from the larger, but thin and eroded upland fields. Paul and Rosie appeared to be starting over for the fourth time.

Building a Garden Fence

Paul and Norbert rambled through the woods searching for dens in which to set traps to control any wild varmints. In the process, they found a couple of sites where a previous owner had made whiskey. There was also an excavation where a mining company had searched for the tar-containing rock that they later mined in the Black Rock Holler south of the Tar Hill Store. Paul's mother had grown up walking these hills. She had driven the oxen pulling the sled with wooden barrels collecting maple sap.

As they walked through the woods, Paul was taking account of the dead chestnut trees that he could cut and drag to the house. The Chestnut trees had been killed by blight, but their tall, straight trunks were still sound. They could easily be split into pickets for a new garden fence.

Norbert held one end of the two-man crosscut saw as they cut several trees. The bark had already fallen from most of the dead trees, allowing Paul to choose the trees with the straightest grain for splitting into pickets. After the team dragged the dead trees to the house, they were cut into logs nearly four feet long, with Norbert again manning one end of the crosscut saw. The short logs were then split into halves with iron wedges and a sledge hammer. Paul used a froe (a riving tool) and a mallet to split the halves into pickets about one inch thick and three to four inches wide.

The small logs and the smaller ends were cut into fence posts. Using a new spool of smooth wire, he wove the several stacks of pickets between two strands of wire at both the top and the bottom ends of the pickets. He tied the fence to the posts. The cracks between the pickets were limited to about one inch, tight enough to keep rabbits, groundhogs and chickens out of the garden. Paul would soon build a gate wide enough to let any of the farm equipment pass through. A garden of about one acre was fenced, large enough for both an early and a late garden.

This old farm had no brooder house for the chickens, so the purchase of chicks was delayed until the weather was warm enough to house them outside. Paul bought a roll of light chicken wire and built a temporary fence around a small area in the corner of the yard. For the first couple of weeks, the chicks were brought inside the house during the night. The floor of the room was covered with empty fertilizer bags and a small circle of fencing, the same fence as used outside, was built to limit the chicks to a small area in the room.

The conditions under which Paul and Rosie found themselves were similar to those found four years before on the Whitfill farm. The significant differences were the four room house, the three children and the short distance to church and school. Another very significant difference was the absence of the positive attitude and support of their previous landlord, Joe Esker Conder.

Grandpa Edward's Visit

On Christmas Eve, Paul and Norbert were cutting stove-wood from the woodpile. Norbert supported his end of the saw while Paul did most of the pushing and pulling. After they had cut several small logs on the saw rack, Paul split the bolts while Norbert hauled the wood to the back porch in his red wagon. They were too busy to notice a visitor riding down the dirt road on his horse, so both were surprised when someone yelled "Merry Christmas!"

Grandpa Edward, Rosie's father dismounted from Old Prince and began helping Norbert load his wagon. When the wagon was loaded, he took two small brown paper bags from his coat pocket and set them on the wood. "Give these to your mother. She will know what to do with them," he said.

Norbert rushed into the house to give the bags to his mother. They were a bag each of orange slices and chocolate drops from the glass candy case in Drake's store at Tar Hill. Rosie explained that Edward was kind to everyone. At Christmas or Easter, he also gave smoked hams from his smokehouse to less fortunate relatives for their holiday dinner.

A Soldier Visits

Rosie's brother, Sylvester Herbert, had been drafted into the army in the spring. When he finished his basic training, he returned home for a couple of weeks and came to visit Rosie and the children, wearing his dress military suit and shoes. After walking the dirt roads, his black shoes were dusty, quite like the farm shoes he had worn in the past. He was quiet and thoughtful, preferring to talk to Rosie rather than play with the kids.

After a short visit, Herbert returned home, again walking the dirt road. He and Rosie would exchange a few letters about his experiences, including the time he was in the hospital for an appendectomy. He would not return home until the end of the war with Japan in the Pacific.

The First School Picnic

At the end of Norbert's first year at St. Paul School, a school picnic was planned. The first grade students were included in the adventurous outing into the woods beside a fresh water spring. The spring was in the farthest NW corner of the Steve Harris farm near Meeting Creek. After Mass at the Church, the students walked single file west on St. Paul Road to the Harris Lane. They walked past Steve and Egart Harris' farms and headed North through the woods to the spring.

The Blue Goose bus followed later with blocks of ice, tubs of soft drinks and bags of wieners, buns and marshmallows. All of the older boys were needed to carry the food and drinks through the woods to the remote picnic site. A fire was built to boil a kettle of water to cook the wieners. Some of the boys, using their pocket knives, cut dozens of green sticks to roast the marshmallows. Egart had helped by previously hauling a sled load of dry poles to burn in the fire.

When everything was organized, the fun began. A ball game was started in the nearby pasture. Several of the boys liked to climb trees or explore the creek banks. Sack races and sprints were organized. Some children preferred to poke at the fire and stir the pot of wieners. Some of the tree climbers were reprimanded for climbing too high, bending and breaking the young trees. Others were reprimanded for removing fishing poles from the creek banks because the poles had been set by the local fishermen to catch catfish. They were checked daily, usually in the early morning, and their fish removed.

Most of the farm children were amused by these risky behaviors. The less adventurous students were disturbed because they were out of their familiar environment.

The long walk home, out of the woods and up the hill, carrying the empty bottles, tubs, pots etc was tiresome. The paper plates and cups had been collected and burned in the fire. Water was carried for quenching the fires. Children who had been so enthusiastic in the morning…singing, shouting and screaming with excitement…were now docile and inattentive.

Visiting Grandma Janie

A few days after school closed for the summer vacation, Paul took Norbert to Mount Hebron to spend a week or more with Janie, his Grandmother. Her youngest son, David, and his young family had moved away after Ike died, so Janie now lived alone.

The house with no small children, no toys and no playmates was uninteresting. Janie invited Jean Miller, a neighbor girl, to play with Norbert. She was the only daughter of the closest neighbor and a couple of years older than Norbert. They explored the orchard, the hen house, the barn and the garden. They found that the June apples were getting ripe, so they climbed the tree and shook several apples to the ground. Grandma Janie sliced the apples, added sugar and pan-fried the apples for dinner. On another day Norbert was given permission to visit Jean's house. Most of the time that day was spent swinging on the rope swing suspended from a tree in the yard.

A few nights later, a summer storm with bright lightning, loud thunder and high winds woke Janie and Norbert. She organized an altar with a crucifix, a Bible, holy water and a lighted candle. Then she went through the house praying aloud and sprinkling everything with holy water. She and Norbert knelt and prayed the Rosiery until the storm passed. Norbert wondered if a lightning strike had been the cause of the fire that had destroyed the Clark house twenty years before.

A Shopping Experience

Samuel was three years old in the fall when the family moved to the old farm. He could now go with Paul and Norbert to Leitchfield on business. He also enjoyed the wedge of hoop cheese or the ring of pickled bologna, the Orange Crush and the soda crackers, all eaten in the farm wagon on the way home. He sometimes got tired during the rushed visits to the stores around town, so Paul carried him on his back.

The Big 7 Store offered farm equipment and hand tools, packaged foods and livestock feeds, farm clothing and dresses or suits. You could buy everything from a straight razor to a farm wagon. It was a multi-level store of multi-departments in an old depot town.

A new hoop of the dark yellow cheese was approximately two feet in diameter, probably weighing nearly fifty pounds. The experienced attendant cut a wedge to the request of the customer.

Paul had been coming to the store since his family's farmhouse burned twenty years before. He had visited the Big 7 with his older brother, Bernard, who bought a straight razor to replace the one that had burned in the house fire. So he was now introducing Samuel to the traditions of the Big 7 Store.

Uncle Jim Riley

During the summer, Paul's Uncle Jim Riley Langley passed the house several times with his fishing poles. Although he lived closer to Clifty Creek, he liked to fish in Meeting Creek where he had fished when he was a boy.

Jim Riley knew where a family of soft shelled turtles lived in the creek. When the sand in the bottom land was dry and hot, the turtles dug a hole in the sand and laid their eggs. Jim Riley would catch the turtles before they returned to the water. When Paul questioned his uncle about the wisdom of killing the female turtles, he assured Paul that he had caught turtles from the creek since he was a boy.

Another Move

About the time the corn was ready to harvest, they were told that they would have to move again. Tony Clark, the owner of the farm, had been laid off from his job and planned to move his family back to the farm for the winter.

11

THE JIM SMALLWOOD FARM

Moving Gets Difficult

Rosie's Aunt Maggie Smallwood and her husband, Jim, lived in Hardin County. Their farm was located near the farm of Uncle John and Aunt Dora where Rosie and Paul had lived six years before. Aunt Maggie and Uncle Jim decided that they could no longer farm the large, rough hill farm with draft horses. If Paul and Rosie would move to the farm, Jim would rent a house and move to Big Clifty near their church and the grocery stores. Paul could move his family into their house on the farm.

Paul's first job was to move the family. He again hired Wavy Drake with his large cattle truck to move all the household items quickly. He moved the animals by walking across Meeting Creek at Tood's Ford and then through the creek bottoms and the woods for the three miles to the farm. The corn, the fodder and the tobacco were moved gradually as the corn was gathered. The market hogs and the frying roosters had been sold. The brood sow in a wooden hog box and the laying hens in the chicken box were moved in the new Owensboro Wagon on the day after the furniture was moved. The two milk cows with rope halters followed, tied to the wagon. On the third day the two smaller hogs intended for slaughter were moved in the hog box crowded between the smaller farm and garden equipment. The gradual move continued for several weeks.

When Paul gathered the corn from the field, he shoveled Tony's one-third share into the crib. The other two-thirds was hauled to the Smallwood farm daily as it was picked. Getting up early in the morning and working until late in the evening, Paul could pick and transport two loads of corn from Tony's fields to the Smallwood farm. Both Paul and the young team were extended to their limits. Norbert, now in the second grade, sometimes walked from the school to help Paul pick the corn, riding home on the wagon.

After the corn was harvested, the fodder was piled high on the wagon and tied securely with ropes. Later when the tobacco was damp and ready to strip, it was moved to the new farm.

Christmas 1943

Paul stripped the tobacco and shipped it to market where it sold shortly before Christmas. Paul was at the auction barn when it was sold and he used the trip to finish his Christmas shopping. When he returned to the farm, he had bought a bag of oranges and a bushel of Wolf River apples, the largest of all varieties. They were snow white inside and were juicy, crisp and tasty. Paul said that Santa had sent these early for Christmas.

On Christmas morning, the family was surprised with a few more presents that Santa had delivered. Norbert got his first toothbrush and Martina got a rag doll with homemade clothes.

Paul had overhauled the rusty red wagon with a new wooden box that he had built in the driveway of the barn. The wagon was

Samuel's, but Norbert could use it to haul wood for the stoves. Rosie made a pan of fudge that would be shared by everyone and Christmas dinner with the smoked ham, the Irish potato salad, canned green beans and apple cobbler provided a festive celebration. Rosie and Paul considered this their most celebrated Christmas since their marriage eleven years before.

Springtime Wildlife Adventures

The new farm was an adventure for a second grader. Jim and Maggie in their old age had not farmed the rough, hilly farm for several years. Weeds, briars and bushes had grown uncontrolled even over the yard and garden. In the large orchard with many varieties of apples and peaches, ripe fruit would drop to the ground and be lost in the underbrush.

Skunks, opossums, foxes, groundhogs, hawks and snakes lived everywhere around the farm, even under the house. The large barn with wide sheds for tobacco, hay and fodder was an interesting place for children to explore. The chicken house with three sections for roosting, laying and raising baby chicks was unusual. Fresh water was carried from a spring under a slight hill.

This farm had deep sinkholes and many rock ledges that provided shelter for hibernating animals and snakes. Since the farm had not been cultivated for years, the undergrowth provided shelter for the varmints in the summer and the field mice and low bird nests provided wild food.

Spot was just as excited as Norbert about all these places. Almost daily he discovered a groundhog or a terrapin, an opossum or a big snake. In the spring when the weather was warm, the vipers, poison copperheads, the blacksnakes and other varieties of snakes seemed to be everywhere and were a constant challenge.

Close Encounters with Poison Snakes

Rosie had turned the laying hens out to run freely in the yard and a few of the hens had gotten under the house through a hole in the underpinning. Rosie suspected that they were laying eggs because they came from under the house cackling loudly as they did when they laid an egg in the henhouse. Norbert was instructed to crawl under the house and search for eggs. When he was sure that no hens were under the house, he was to fasten the galvanized underpinning.

In the dim light under the house Norbert could see a nest of white eggs. As he crawled toward them, the dog rushed in front of him barking loudly. Then he saw a large snake lying quietly near the nest. When the dog got between Norbert and the snake, the snake raised its head to the floor above and hissed at the dog. It struck out several times at Spot as he was barking and circling around the snake.

The low space under the floor restricted the snake's movement, so it was not able to extend and strike its full length. Once when it was slow to recoil after a strike, Spot jumped in and grabbed the snake by its neck and started shaking it, snapping the snake. When the snake went limp, Spot dragged the snake outside.

Rosie had been puzzled by the commotion under the floor. When she saw the snake, she yelled, "Norbert! Are you all right?" The snake was a large, poisonous copperhead. It had probably eaten several eggs. Norbert retrieved the remaining eggs cautiously watching for other snakes. Then he carefully closed the hole in the underpinning.

Several other snake encounters occurred during the spring and summer. A large cow snake took up residence in the corn crib. Paul protected this snake because it helped control the rats and mice. Paul also plowed up a poison cottonmouth with a nest of snake eggs when he cultivated the bottomland near the creek. Spot treed an extremely large cow snake in the middle of the road near the freshwater spring, and killed it after Norbert knocked it down with a flat stone. The dead snake extended a foot past the wagon tracks on both sides of the road.

One Saturday afternoon when the family was on the way to Drake's store at Tar Hill, they came upon a knot of snakes in the hot, sandy road in the bottom land. Paul stopped the horses before they reached the snakes. He dismounted from the wagon and walked forward to investigate while the family watched.

There appeared to be two snakes in a fight with each other for their lives. The spread head viper appeared to already be nearly lifeless. The blue racer, a variety of the black snake, was winding tighter and tighter around the defenseless viper. Paul picked up a rock and pitched it on the knot of snakes. The blue racer unknotted and disappeared into the grass beside the road. The viper remained motionless in the road.

One hot summer day when Paul was cultivating corn in the hill field furthest from the house, Norbert was sent to call him to lunch. Spot, ranging ahead of Norbert, started barking at a snake in the middle of the road under the wire gate. The snake extended its head above the dog, hissing loudly and striking its full length. Norbert found a flat rock and pitched it on the snake, and then Spot grabbed the snake and snapped it until it was lifeless.

When Norbert showed the snake to Paul, he identified it as a poisonous copperhead. That snake, with the cottonmouth in the bottomland and the copperhead killed under the house made three poisonous snakes killed on the Smallwood farm.

Varmits versus Chickens

The varmints and hawks also were a constant challenge. When the small chicks were turned outside in the chicken lot or the barn lot, the hawks and the foxes threatened daily. A hawk could swoop into the lots and, in a couple of seconds, fly away with a squawking chick. Periodically, a laying hen would disappear without a trace. At other times, a trail of feathers would lead to a den under a cliff, making it evident from the bones and feathers that a mother fox had fed her pups.

The doors to the chicken houses were closed when the hens and chicks went to roost at twilight. One night about bedtime, Spot started barking by the closed henhouse door. Paul went to investigate. He returned shortly to get the kerosene lantern and the loaded shotgun. Spot was still barking outside the door of the chicken house where three brooding hens were sitting on eggs for hatching.

When Paul opened the door, Spot rushed in. One hen was squawking in the corner. Spot rushed to the nest where the brooding hen had been incubating the eggs and quickly pulled a skunk from the nest. The foul odor from the skunk's spray filled the chicken house. Spot made short work of killing the skunk which had dug a hole under the wall to get to the eggs.

Shortly afterwards, Spot started vomiting. He was very sick and would not eat nor come to his regular bed on the porch. He lay by the side of the road beside a puddle of water. When anyone approached him with a tasty morsel of food, he growled. Since growling was not part of his friendly personality, everyone knew that they should leave him alone.

About the third day, he raised himself to his feet and weakly staggered to the porch. Rosie prepared a small bowl of his favorite brown gravy with a biscuit from breakfast. He ate sparingly for a few days before returning to his friendly energetic self.

A few days after that skunk episode, Norbert found five young skunks playing in the woods by the spring. He ran to the house to get a cardboard box and caught most of the kittens before they escaped into the den. Norbert's plan was to raise the skunks as pets, but Rosie had other plans. She told Norbert to return the skunks to the den. They were old enough to survive in the woods without their mother who obviously had been the thief-in-the-night that Spot had killed in the henhouse.

Adventurous Walk to the School Bus

When the family moved in the fall of 1943, Norbert had to walk from the Hardin County farm to St. Paul Road to catch the school bus. He crossed Meeting Creek by walking on large stones that Paul had placed across the riffle. As the fall rains came and the level of the water increased, Paul took Norbert across the creek on one of the horses and met him in the evening.

To solve the problem of crossing the creek, Paul arranged with Mr. Burkhead, who owned the land on the south side of the creek, to fell a large elm tree across the creek as a foot log. The foot log was located where the creek-banks were highest. When the snow fell and the log was covered with ice, Paul nailed a side rail to the foot log, so Norbert could cross the creek safely. The shortcut across the creek reduced a three-mile walk to the school bus by a half mile.

The trip to the school bus took about forty-five minutes in good weather. Norbert, in his denim overalls, bare footed, carrying his book satchel and his lunch pail, could run downhill. The walk up-hill was slower.

In the winter when the road was snowy or muddy, it took about one hour to reach the bus. Norbert was also slowed by his high-top work shoes, his four-buckle overshoes and his heavy coat buttoned to the neck.

Hosscat Burkhead with his three hounds often hunted in the woods that Norbert traveled to catch the bus. Once, when the hounds were hunting near the road, Norbert climbed a tree to escape them, causing him to miss the bus. He walked the extra two miles to the school, arriving just as the students left the Church from daily Mass.

Norbert often saw a fisherman or a hunter in the woods. They hunted for squirrels or crows and fished for bass and bluegills. In the spring, when the white suckers spawned on the riffles, the fishermen used five-pronged spears to spear the suckers.

Joe "Tick" Langley, a relative of Paul's, was the most versatile and consistent woodsman that Norbert saw in the woods. He trapped for muskrats and mink in season and also gathered nuts from the shagbark hickory and the black walnut trees. In the spring, he located the beds of ginseng on the cool north hillsides in the woods. He watched the ginseng grow and selected the largest, three-pronged plants with the largest roots for harvesting in the fall. Most hunters would have pulled all the plants, eliminating the possibility of a future crop. Joe also dug the large beds of may-apple root and dried them for sale at Sam Terry's hardware store in Big Clifty.

Joe Tick and his wife, Millie, had no children. They lived on a small farm, growing a garden and a small patch of tobacco and comfortably maintained their connection to the past and the present. Norbert enjoyed meeting and talking to Joe Tick about his pursuits in the woods.

Overnight at Grandpa's House

Because Norbert's grandparents, Edward and Mary Alta Milliner, lived near the school bus route, he was given the freedom to decide to stay overnight at their house. If it was raining or snowing, if a thunder cloud appeared in the sky or if the winter weather was too cold,

Norbert went to his grandparent's house. Rosie's youngest sister, Jean, also a second grader, provided extra incentive to make that visit.

Norbert, as the first grandchild, was given special consideration by his grandparents. He could request a goose egg boiled for breakfast or a snack of sweet apple preserves and a slice of butter on a biscuit—and his request would be granted.

Wanting to be helpful, Norbert also helped Jean carry water from the spring and shell corn for the chickens. In the spring, they searched for goose nests hidden in the dead grass or under the leaves in the woods. Granny always made sure that they finished all their homework.

History...An Old Millsite Discovered

Most of the daily trip to the school bus was through the woods traveling up and down the roads north and south of Meeting Creek. The steep farm road had been travelled for generations. Jim Smallwood's ancestors since before the Civil War had travelled this road going to St. Paul Catholic Church, built in 1812. In some areas, the road bed was eroded several feet deep exposing the sandstone ledges. Jim's ancestor, Solomon Smallwood, had built a water powered mill on Meeting Creek. Folklore among the community talked about the old mill, but no one knew where it had been located.

When Paul was plowing the bottom land in the spring, he discovered many large rocks in the ground at the west end of the bottom land. The area was elevated a few feet, slightly above the high water line when the creek flooded. Paul continued to expose these large rocks. He eventually returned to the barnyard to get the sled to haul the rocks from the field. He commented to Norbert, "Looks like

148

there might have been a house here at one time." Some of the rocks looked as if they had been shaped as foundation or chimney stones.

A few years later, when seining in the creek in the same area, the seine hung itself on several even larger rocks in the creek bed. These rocks were of the sculptured, rectangular shape that would have been necessary for building a dam.

At a family reunion in 2008, a descendent of the Smallwood's mentioned that his grandparents had talked about a Smallwood mill. It had been located on the creek on the farm that Paul was renting. The ancestor's name was Solomon Smallwood. Civil War records from the pension department confirmed Solomon's residence in the area in the 1880s. But the only evidence of the existence of the mill were the rocks that Paul hauled to the edge of the fields and the presence of the large rocks in the creek bed.

Going to Church in Winter

The journey to St. Paul Church in the winter was difficult. For Rosie and the small children, it was especially difficult. As the family grew, the small buggy was sold and the new farm wagon was used for such trips.

With a mattress of straw or hay, the family, except Paul the driver, nestled in the wagon bed under the quilts for warmth. The trip of nearly five miles, half of which was up and down rough hilly roads, took more than one hour in good weather. Because of the difficulty, Rosie and the small children seldom went to Sunday Mass in winter.

Paul and Norbert went to the Sunday services riding one of the horses. Bundled in their warmest winter clothes, they could comfortably endure most bad weather. Norbert rode on a burlap bag behind the saddle, his feet dangling loosely at the sides of the horse. In extremely cold weather, his feet in his four-buckle boots became so cold and painful that Paul pulled them up and tucked them under his overcoat. The trip home when the temperature was warmer was usually more comfortable.

Preparing for a New Brother

In early February, 1944, Norbert was told that he would spend the weekend at the Cook's house. Shortly after the Clarks moved to the Smallwood farm, the closest neighbor, the Cooks, had come to visit. Roy and May Cook had two children, Jean and Harold, who were two or three years older than Norbert. After supper Paul saddled Dock and they started to the Cooks' house.

Norbert had not travelled this road north from the farm towards the community of Limp, so after leaving the steep hill and travelling into the woods, the road became mysterious. A large open-pit rock quarry opened to the right of the road. The limestone had been mined leaving tall, straight cliffs on three sides. The bottom of the quarry, level with the road, was covered with snow. Shadows in the semi-darkness of the quarry created a mysterious atmosphere. After passing the quarry and climbing a steep hill out of the woods, the road emerged across the county road in front of the Cooks' farmhouse.

For the remainder of the evening, Norbert worked (for the first time) at a jigsaw puzzle with Jean and Harold. Roy and May would periodically offer a suggestion or pick and place a piece of the puzzle.

In the morning, May prepared a generous breakfast of sausage, eggs, biscuits, gravy and milk, similar to the breakfast Rosie would have prepared at home. Jean, Harold and Norbert went back to the jigsaw puzzle. The puzzle was shortly finished, a farm scene of a red barn with cattle and horses in the barn lot. Next, they brought out a checker board, placing it flat over the puzzle. Harold went outside to help his father around the farm. Norbert had never played checkers, so Jean took the opportunity to teach the game to Norbert. At Norbert's request, Paul later built a checker board for his children.

At about noon, Paul came on the horse to get Norbert. The large rock quarry was less mysterious in the daylight. The snow on the quarry floor had begun melting, creating shallow puddles.

Paul told Norbert that he had a surprise at home. When they got home, Norbert had a new brother. Grandma Janie, Paul's mother who had been the midwife, was ready for Paul to take her home. The next day, Paul would bring Hershel Drury's daughter Annie to stay the ten days that Rosie was required to stay in bed. The baby was named Daniel Edward.

A Spring Outing

When spring arrived, Rosie was eager to escape the winter doldrums. She had not been beyond the chicken house or the barn since Christmas. Paul, who was ready for his weekly trip to Drake's store at Tar Hill to sell eggs and cream and to grind corn for the milk cows, agreed that Rosie should come along. She might also find material at the store to sew a new dress for Martina or the new baby.

When they arrived at the store, Rosie's sister, Sarah Marie, with her cousins, Mary Ann and Betty Jean were there. As young teenagers, they were excited about the new baby. Rosie suggested that the girls come home with her and stay overnight.

The girls would first have to ask their parents, so Sarah Marie ran the half mile home to get permission from her mother. Mary Ann and Betty Jean, who lived close by, returned quickly with permission and a few clothes to wear to Church the next morning.

The wagon was full on the way home. The girls sat on the bags of crushed corn and dangled their legs over the sides. After they crossed Meeting Creek and started following the hillside around the edge of the bottomland, someone spotted a morel mushroom.

Everyone jumped off the wagon and began searching for the mushrooms. They filled the egg basket and the cream pail. The dinner at home that evening was planned around the morels. The early garden leaf-lettuce, the radishes and the green onions balanced the pan-fried mushrooms. Fried morels, instead of bacon or sausage, were also served with scrambled eggs the next morning for breakfast. When the girls returned to their families at Church the next morning, the Clark family truly missed them.

A New Cow

Paul decided to buy another milk cow in the spring. She would produce another veal calf and add to the cream sales. The additional milk could also be used to feed a few more market hogs.

The cow that he bought was a young Holstein who had been raised since a calf by Jessie Clark, who lived south of St. Paul cemetery. Paul led the cow home with a rope halter. Compared to the small Jersey milk cows, this cow was large and colorful. The contrasting black and white color set her apart from the dull brown or brindle Jerseys. She was easy to milk and extremely gentle compared to the nervous Jerseys. Norbert gave the cow so much attention that Paul said that he could call her 'his cow.' and he was responsible for milking the cow night and morning.

The additional cream supply meant that the cream pail was filled more often. The cream and the eggs could be sold at the general store in Hardin County at the community of Limp. Paul still had to visit Drake's store at Tar Hill to grind corn for the milk cows. When school was out for the summer and Paul was more involved with cultivating the crops, Norbert was given the responsibility of carrying the cream and eggs to Puckett's store in Limp, a store that also was a post office.

The journey to the store was longer than two miles. Whether he was carrying cream or eggs, Norbert, at age eight, stopped often to rest. His shoulders would become tired or his fingers cramped around the handles of the cream pail. He often set the pail or basket down beside the road for a few minutes to rest his shoulders and fingers.

Periodically, Norbert would buy a few groceries at the store. This meant he had a load such as five or ten pounds of sugar, a bag of insecticide or a pail of lard to carry home. Mr. or Mrs. Puckett, who were responsible for all the operations in the store and the post office, subtracted the price of the groceries from the money received from the cream and eggs. Norbert stuffed the earned money into his pocket and headed towards the enclosed glass case of candy. A Baby Ruth candy bar was the usual reward for his trip to the store.

Planting Watermelons

After the spring garden was planted, a section of the large fenced garden was selected for planting watermelons. The sandy soil was plowed, harrowed and dragged until the soil was pulverized. Paul planned to plant the melons in a pattern with hills on the corners of a ten foot square. He stepped and marked the ground. With a single-shovel plow, he laid the pattern for fifty hills. At the intersection of the furrows, he dug a hole about a foot deep. Into each hole he shoveled about a half bushel of rotted horse manure that he had hauled from the barn on the farm sled. The manure in the hole was packed and covered with soil to a height of about six inches. Six seeds were planted about one inch deep distributed over the surface of the hill. If all of these seeds germinated, they would be thinned to three or four plants per hill.

When they ripened, Paul could take a wagon load of the large tasty Klickley Sweet melons to the grocery stores to sell to the Saturday crowds. Everyone knew about the sweet, crisp taste of the Klickley Sweets.

To Church with Small Children

As the weather improved in the spring, Rosie, with her two babies, again started going to Church on Sunday. Her preparation for the excursion of nearly four hours included several cotton diapers, wet washcloths and small towels. On one particular Sunday, the preparation was not sufficient to provide for the trip home, so Rosie suggested that before they drove over the hill into the woods on their way home, they stop at Mr. and Mrs. Burkhead's house to replenish the supplies.

Mr. and Mrs. Burkhead's son had married Rosie's next younger sister, Theresa. They were Protestants and a church of their denomination did not exist in the community, so they were somewhat isolated in the predominately Catholic community. When the Clark family arrived, it was near lunchtime and Mrs. Burkhead had already set the table for herself and her husband. When the problem with the babies had been solved, Mr. and Mrs. Burkhead strongly begged Rosie and Paul to stay for dinner. They could quickly fry another pone of cornbread and open a can of green beans, and Mrs. Burkhead had baked a blackberry cobbler large enough for both families. To the disappointment of the children, Rosie and Paul politely apologized for their sudden intrusion. They proceeded over the hill into the woods on their way to the Smallwood farm near the Limp community in Hardin County.

Burning the Underbrush

Around the farm in several places were swales (low and marshy land) and sinkholes. One depression was in the large barn lot itself. Neighbors familiar with the farm said that it had previously been a large sink hole that Uncle Jim Smallwood had filled with stones from the fields. Using a pond scraper pulled by the horses, he had created a pond. The run-off from the hills on three sides of the pond provided sufficient water for livestock except in the dry months of August and September.

Because the farm had not had livestock for several years, the wild grass and briars had accumulated on the hills around the pond. Paul had mentioned that the dead grass and briars needed to be burned, but so far other jobs had taken priority and the dead residue still was there.

One day, the afternoon was warm; the weather was dry and the wind was calm. Paul had said that these were the conditions necessary for burning the dead materials, so Norbert approached Rosie with the question, "May I burn the brush in the barn lot?" After a little begging, she agreed that the conditions were ideal and gave him two matches to start the fire. He could twist the dead grass to use as a torch to spread the fire. Fortunately, most of the dead residue was on the north side of the pond opposite the barn.

As the fire spread and reached the dense undergrowth, the flames and the heat intensified reaching several feet into the air. Then, as always happens when the heat increases, the wind increased. The fire in the high wind started spreading rapidly up the hill towards a hayfield.

Norbert rushed to the house to warn Rosie of the catastrophe. Rosie grabbed the ax as she ran past the woodpile. On her way to the fire, she cut a red cedar bush about six feet tall to use as a broom to beat the fire down and sweep the burning grass into the previously burned area. Within a couple of minutes, she had the fire under control. Norbert stood at the edge of the yard with the younger children and watched as Rosie returned to the house.

She explained that the wind had been the problem and sent Norbert to pick up the ax that she had left on the hill. Paul explained later that the fire would probably have died out when it reached the green hay field, but no explanation reduced the excitement or the potential danger in Norbert's mind.

Six New Calves

Paul sold three veal calves that summer and Wavy Drake hauled the calves to the Bourbon Stockyard in Louisville. Paul told Wavy to buy a couple of Jersey heifer calves if the price was right. Wavy attended the auctions almost weekly as he hauled the farmers' livestock to market. He knew the prices and Paul trusted him to make the right decision.

When Wavy returned in the evening, he brought six Jersey heifer calves. He explained that he bought the six calves for the same price that he would have paid for two calves. Since no one at the auction bid on the calves, Wavy's opening bid was the only bid. He would take some of the calves back to the market the following week if Paul chose not to keep them. Or, since Paul had plenty of pasture and a good hay crop, he could feed the calves through the winter and sell them the next spring for a good profit.

Paul kept the calves. The next summer he bred four of the most promising heifers to double his herd of milk cows. Then he sold two of the most nervous and skittish heifers back into the market.

School Days 1944

In September, Norbert started the third grade. His third-grade classmates were the experienced students in the three-class room. Sister Mary Estelle now had two years of experience in managing the large room.

St. Paul School was expanding. A third room was added and, each year, another high school class would be added until a full high school was established.

Shortly after school started, Norbert brought a letter home from the teacher. It was typewritten and mimeographed in rather business-like way. The letter explained that students were expected to wear shoes to school. Attending school bare footed as Norbert and many of the farm boys were accustomed to doing was now forbidden.

Rosie ordered a new pair of shoes, a pair of blue jeans and a new belt from the Sears Roebuck Catalog. She would still sew his shirts and underwear herself.

Recess play was simple. Marbles, played according to several different designs and under several sets of rules, were popular games for the third grade boys. Norbert convinced Rosie to buy him a bag of 25 new marbles. After a few weeks, Norbert had filled both pockets of his new pants with his winnings. The boys who lost all their marbles turned to games of mumbly-peg using their pocket knives.

The girls usually jumped rope or played hopscotch. The older girls taught the younger girls to jump the rope and to skip on one foot. Some of the girls brought their dolls to school and played with them at recess and dinner.

At about this time, the men of the parish scheduled a workday to build swings and seesaws, and Paul participated. They set tall red cedar posts in the ground and hung chains from steel pipes. Seesaws were built using short posts and short steel pipes. In fact, all of the play equipment was built of steel and heavy wooden boards. After a few bumps, students learned to recognize the danger and play other games at a distance from the heavy equipment.

Author's Note

In 2006 I visited the old Smallwood farm where I had lived as an adventurous eight year old boy 63 years before. The old farm was isolated by two or three miles of land in all directions, so a walk to the school bus was three miles through the woods, down the hill, across the creek, up another hill. The dirt roads when dry could be travelled by a car but the rains had eroded the dirt, washing ditches in the middle of the road. My main concerns on this trip were, "Are the roads dry?" and "Will the tires survive the many stones?"

After opening two wire gates and driving across a hillside field, we arrived at the old farm house. It appeared as the house of my memory, but weathered and unkempt. No one had lived there for many years. Originally, it had been a large two-room log house. When we lived there, it had been overhauled with side rooms, weatherboarding and porches.

The barn, the garden, the orchards, the crib and the outhouse were gone. The large chicken house strategic to our food supply was still there. The hill in the front of the house was covered with a million daffodils. The road in the front of the house, over the hill, to Smallwood Ford at Meeting Creek was impassable. (This old road probably dated back to the original settlers.) Most of the farm fields, too rough for modern farm equipment, had been converted to pastureland. The unfenced, fertile bottom land was covered with small trees.

I remembered the farm as rugged and productive, a farm where our happy family had lived. My appropriate response was the following song.

RETURN TO THE LAND

And I return to the land,

The land that I understand

To the good land where I lived long ago.

I travel back roads never paved,

Open gates down the lane;

I know happiness, my boyhood, my home.

And I walk 'round the old farm,

The house, the old barn;

I see the roses that bloomed long ago.

I see old friends passing by;

Hawks soar high in blue skies;

I know the hardships that made this land grow.

I see my parents so dear

And our good neighbors lived near,

And with relatives helped build this land.

Hard lives of work, hard lives of toil;

Hard lives they lived on this soil;

These poor farmers who helped build this land.

I see the toys that Dad made;

I hear the music he played;

I hear the voices who sang long ago.

I know the laughter, the cheer,

I know the heartaches, the tears;

I know the sweet dreams that made their love grow.

I see the mule, the old dog;

I see the chickens and fat hog;

I see the kittens that played 'round the barn.

My happy boyhood, long gone,

But the memories live on,

The fondest of memories, a song.

Yes, for each other they cared

And all their hard lives they shared;

Their good lives, they shared with their friends.

And if sometime they could return

Would they remember and yearn

For the good life that I understand.

-Song by Norbert Clark

12

ANOTHER UNEXPECTED MOVE

Moving Close to Church and School

Paul and Rosie, unhappy with the remote location of the Smallwood Farm, were continuously attentive to the possibility of moving closer to school and church. With a young family rapidly approaching school age, their location was critical.

Harve Smallwood, the brother of Jim Smallwood, was rearranging his living conditions as Jim and Maggie had done the year before. He had sold the farm to his son-in-law, Tony Clark, Paul's cousin; but Tony, during the war, was working in industry and living with his family in Louisville. Tony made arrangements for Paul to move his family to the farm.

The farm was near school and church. The students playing in the playground at school could be heard in the living room at home. Norbert could run home for lunch and return to school with time to play a few games of marbles.

The five room house with a dormer and a porch across the front was a major improvement over any of the houses where they had lived. The barn, the cellar, the smoke house and the chicken house were up-to-date and well maintained. They included a warm brooder house for the two hundred chicks that would be sold as frying roosters. The large fenced garden included a few modern peach trees and grapevines of three varieties. The garden with the multiplier onions and the rhubarb along the fence was ready for plowing and planting.

Clearing Another Field

Tony, knowing Paul's experience at reclaiming old farms, arranged with him to clear a large north field that Harve had ignored for several years. The bushes, some 10 feet tall, and the briar patches were similar to those Paul had experienced on the Whitfill farm. The arrangement provided that Paul could keep all the corn that he produced on the field.

Paul, knowing that he would need help clearing such a large field, hired his nephew, Lennie Fraze. Lennie had just finished the eighth grade and he approached the project with light hearted enthusiasm. Paul required that the bushes be cut about six inches into the ground. This would help kill the roots and make plowing easier. The blackberry briars and the broom sage were burned in place, since the turning plow would cut through the roots. The bushes and the briars were piled and burned for plant beds for tobacco and garden plants.

At the end of the week, Lennie stuffed his pay of ten dollars into his pocket and left the farm in a run. He was anticipating a stop at the country store since this was the first money he had earned. Lennie would repeat the week three or four times until the job was completed.

Planting Corn

When Paul had plowed the field, Rosie's father and brother came to help plant the corn. Joe Ed would drag and harrow the field with one team. Paul and Grandpa Edward would plant the corn one row at a time with a one-row Camel drill. Paul laid-off the rows with a single-shovel plow. Grandpa Edward followed with the drill planting seed corn and fertilizer.

Grandpa Edward was confident that Norbert, who would be nine years old in June, could manage the corn drill. Doc, the most gentle horse, would follow the furrow and Norbert could balance the drill. It consisted of one large diameter wheel of mechanical gears, and two paddles in the rear for covering the corn. The gears activated the planting mechanism distributing the seed corn and the fertilizer.

The hardest part of this work was turning the drill at the end of the row. Guiding the horse through the 180° turn would be difficult. If Norbert could guide the horse to make half of the turn, he could tilt the drill the remaining half-turn and proceed in the opposite direction. After a few attempts and a little help from Grandpa, Norbert could balance and turn the drill. Grandpa was then free to work with anyone who needed help.

Good Neighbors

When Rosie and Paul moved to the Harve Smallwood farm, they lived less than one quarter mile from Harve's brother, Clay, his wife, Mattie and their two sons, Sid and Todd. Clay and his family owned a battery radio. In the winter and spring of 1945, Clay and Mattie invited Paul and Rosie with the family to listen to the evening war news. The two families sat silently listening as Gabriel Heater and Lowell Thomas described the progress of the Allied troops in Europe and the South Pacific. Their stern, solemn voices added to the suspense. Both families had close relatives and friends in these wars. The silent walk home with the kerosene lantern, wondering about the safety of Rosie's two brothers and Paul's cousins was puzzling to the children.

Farm Life Improves

Paul's and Rosie's lives were gradually improving. They would have seven milk cows when the heifers calved in the spring. The milk cows, bred to a neighbor's Herford bull would produce first class veal calves. Projecting the additional milk, Paul added a second brood sow. This would result in four litters of pigs, totaling about thirty market hogs. The extra cream and the eggs provided a weekly paycheck.

Paul bought a cream separator to process the large volume of milk from the seven cows. The separator extracted the cream immediately from the warm milk. Waiting for the cream to separate from the milk was no longer a problem. The skimmed milk, thickened with high protein tankage (food supplement), rushed the hogs to market in about six months. Additional milk was thickened with chick starter or laying mash and fed to the chickens.

The expenses for the self-sufficient family were minimal. Rosie sewed most of the shirts and patched the pants until they were thread-bare. The garden, the fruit trees, the grape vines and the blackberries provided fruits and vegetables for daily consumption. The excess was canned, dried or preserved for the next winter. An old hen for a pot of chicken and dumplings, when the pork from the previous winter had all been eaten, filled out the menu. Two large hogs would be killed again in the winter.

Paul built everything that could be built of wood. He built a larger hayrack that reduced the trips from the hayfield to the barn or the haystack by half. At Christmas, he built a sleek, fast sled for the children. On split hickory runners, the sled was so fast that the children were afraid to ride it. Loaded with firewood for the house, the sled was still easy to pull.

Haircuts with Music

At the Harve Smallwood farm, Paul was too far from Tar Hill to return to Hosscat's house for a haircut. Lawrence, Joe, Azora and Little Bill Drury, a family of bachelor brothers and a sister, lived across Meeting Creek in Hardin County. Joe, the middle brother, cut the hair of the family and the neighbors. Since the Drurys walked past the Smallwood farm house on their way to St. Paul Church, Joe and Paul agreed to trade haircuts.

The Drurys were also musicians. Lawrence, the oldest, was a left-handed fiddler. Azora played the organ. Joe joined in where needed. Little Bill was handicapped, but he jigged to all of the music. The Drurys learned that Paul also played the fiddle, so after his first trip to the Drurys for a haircut, Paul always had to take his fiddle for a music session.

The handicapped brother, Little Bill, was a comical character who wore his black rubber boots and an old suit-coat winter and summer. He liked to talk and laugh and express his simple philosophies.

Little Bill often went hunting for squirrels under a large hickory nut tree. A neighbor, out hunting in the same woods, knew of that hickory nut tree and its generous crop of nuts. When he approached the tree, several squirrels were eating the nuts. Little Bill was sitting under the tree watching the squirrels. The neighbor quietly approached Little Bill, whose gun was leaning against the tree beside him, and pointed to the squirrels. Little Bill whispered, "I only have one shell. I might want to go hunting tomorrow." This simple response was typical of Little Bill's life philosophy.

One More Time

When the war ended in the summer of 1945, industry rapidly converted to manufacturing domestic products. Tony, who had returned to work at Reynolds Metal during the war, was again laid off. His only option was to return to his farm, but, since Tony also owned the old Langley Farm where Paul and Rosie had lived briefly, he agreed to sell that farm to Paul.

In early 1946, Paul and Rosie moved for the 10th and last time since 1932 when they were married.

Tony had overhauled the log house in which Paul and Rosie had lived previously. It looked more modern with new windows, a new galvanized roof and white weatherboard siding. The stone chimney on the south end of the house had been dismantled and replaced with a brick flue. The inside was covered with sheet rock and the ceiling was covered with tongue-and-groove pine. A new barn with a wide driveway, a hay loft and a corn crib had been built.

The old log barn still stood across the road from the house. Paul quickly dismantled the barn and used the materials to build a chicken house. Despite some improvements, if it was compared to the Condor and the Smallwood farms, the renovated farm and its living conditions was inferior. Water still had to be carried from a spring under a steep hill. There was no plumbing. The crooked dirt road was impassable by car much of the year. The productivity of the eroded farm land was more meager than that of any farm they had rented.

After fourteen years of marriage and ten moves, Rosie and Paul were permanently settled, but they would still live using the skills they had learned from their ancestors.

13
SLOW BUT STEADY PROGRESS

After Paul and Rosie bought and moved back to the old Langley farm, they continued to make financial progress. The farm loan from the Big Clifty Bank was paid off in about three years, helped by the "nest egg" they had accumulated during the last prosperous years of WWII.

The children walked to the St. Paul Parochial School. Lowell Patrick, their fifth child, was born in the spring of 1946. Christine Agnes and Kathleen Marie followed at two-year intervals.

Paul was able to earn extra money working on a construction crew building housing at Fort Knox for the families of soldiers returning from WWII. Rosie bought a hand–operated washing machine with a manual clothes wringer to wash the increasing amount of clothing from the growing family. When this machine wore out after a couple of years, she bought a used washing machine powered by a gasoline engine.

Rosie raised a large garden and preserved, canned or dried enough food to feed the family throughout the year. Combined with the two hogs slaughtered each winter, the eggs and the occasional chicken from the laying hens or frying roosters, and a generous supply of milk, the family was well fed.

History Repeated

The cool fresh water spring from which Grandma Janie had carried water to the workmen who built their log cabin in 1880 was used as the family refrigerator. During warm weather, after milking the cows night and morning, a gallon of milk for drinking and cooking was stored in the spring. The old hen or the frying rooster, killed on Saturday afternoon and planned for Sunday dinner, was placed in a gallon jug of salt water and stored in the spring. The butter, subject to melting in the hot summer kitchen, was also stored in the spring.

The cool spring water that flowed uninterrupted during the hot summer months was the perfect substitute for refrigeration. The inconvenience of its location under a steep hill far from the house meant that the children made many trips down and up the hill, but this free cooling was used until electricity was installed in 1958.

Paul used the money he earned working in Fort Knox to hire a well digger to bore a well in the back yard, but the attempt was not successful. The house was built on a ridge at the top of a steep hill several hundred feet in elevation, and the cracked rock structure did not hold water. After boring about two hundred feet without success, Paul's money was exhausted and he discontinued the project. That well drilling project was a disappointment added to other setbacks.

Slowly Adjusting

In order to expand the farm operation, Paul rented land from neighbors. He cut hay and planted a field of corn on the farm of Miss

Rose Portman. The yields from these fields were much improved compared to the yields from the thin soil of the Langley farm. The extra corn and hay was fed to the expanding herd of cows and the increasing number of market hogs.

During the early summer, while working on the Portman farm, Paul came down with malaria. He was in bed for about a month with alternating fevers and chills. Quinine, the medicine prescribed by Dr. Phelps, helped him recover. The source? His cousin and close friend, Bennie Johnson had fought in the jungles of Burma during WWII, and had returned home with malaria.

Rosie's brothers and their neighbors, the Portman boys, organized a work day to cultivate Paul's corn fields. Six or seven men and boys with their horses and their single and double shovel plows followed by harrows, were able to cultivate the corn in one day.

Farming Practices Change

After WWII. the viability of the Clark's family farm rapidly decreased. The prices paid to farmers for sour cream, from which butter was made, and hogs, on which Paul had depended, rapidly declined after the war. Margarine, produced primarily from soybean oil, was advertised as healthier than butter. The value of the veal calves, a convenient byproduct of the cream production, rapidly declined. Feeder calves of the mixed beef breeds were more in demand to supply the expanding commercial feed lots. The money realized from the cream, the few eggs and the frying roosters that had provided continuity to the family money supply during the war decreased rapidly. Large commercial chicken farms for producing fryers and eggs rendered the small chicken operation obsolete for the subsistence farmer raising a large family.

Paul slowly adjusted to the changes. He rented land on which to produce the added corn necessary for raising more market hogs. Instead of selling the heifer calves from beef-type Herford bulls as prime veal calves, these calves were saved to produce a beef-type herd of cows. The aging Jersey milk cows were slowly sold and replaced with the half-breed beef-type heifers for producing feeder calves.

Tobacco provided the most dependable income for the small farmer, but the quantity of tobacco raised by each farmer was controlled by a 'base system'. The only way for a farmer to increase his tobacco base was to buy more land. Paul bought an additional forty acres of land adjacent to the Langley farm, more than doubling his tobacco base. This land that was more level and more fertile than the land of the Langley farm was also more productive for raising extra corn and hay.

The farm, as the primary business in support of the growing family, was given priority in all financial decisions. Old fences were replaced. A larger corn crib was built.

The mud road, impassable much of the year, was ignored. The weatherboarding on the old house was rapidly losing its paint. Water for cooking and drinking was still carried from the spring by the children.

In the absence of electricity and transportation, daily routines on the old farm continued in the same patterns practiced when Paul and Rosie had first moved the family there in 1942. Hand labor supported by the labor of the team of horses was used to cultivate the garden, the tobacco, the corn and to harvest the hay. When the dry weather limited the hay crop, corn fodder was harvested to feed the livestock. If the corn crop was also reduced by the dry weather, the pigs that were intended to be sold at slaughter weight were sold as lightweight feeder pigs. Flexibility and constant adjustment were necessary for survival.

Cousins Visit for the Summer

During the summer of 1950, Pete and Clem, the teenage sons of Paul's oldest brother, Lawrence, spent most of their summer vacation with Paul and Rosie's family.

They went swimming almost every day in Able's Hole in Meeting Creek. Paul built a diving board on the bank of the swimming hole. The boys had bragged about how well they could dive in the city pool in Richmond, Indiana where they lived, so they were happy being able to dive in the country. Paul also built two long bows from seasoned red cedar so that the boys could pretend they were Indian hunters in the woods.

When the farm work was under control, Paul took the brothers with Norbert and Samuel in the farm wagon to visit his brother David and wife Ann's family. They forded Clifty Creek at the site of the old Pool's mill and continued to travel the back country dirt roads past the Fraze and Mattingly farms. David and Ann were renting and farming the land of Ann's brother, Virgil. This was an adventurous journey for the boys who lived in the city.

Subsidizing the Small Farm System

Paul recognized the financial difficulty inherent in the declining family-farm system. In 1951, he took a job working in the foundry at

International Harvester in Louisville, and bought his first car, a 1949 Chevrolet. During the winter and spring when the mud roads were impassable, the car was left at the entrance of the dirt road three quarters of a mile from the house. Going to Sunday Mass in the farm wagon was no longer necessary.

Paul rode the Kentucky bus line to and from Louisville on the weekend. He lived with relatives during the week riding the city bus to and from work. This arrangement was similar to that of eleven years before when Paul had worked at the Seventh Street Tobacco Warehouse. At the age of 40, Paul soon gained experience and confidence driving the car, so he was able to abandon the bus systems and drive the car to Louisville and to work in the city.

The farm operation was scaled back to a level manageable by Rosie and the older children. The traditional functions stayed: planting a large garden along with the canning, preserving, drying and pickling were still accomplished by Rosie. The hogs were killed and the sausage canned. The brooding hens were set producing a few fryers and replacements for the old egg laying hens. The hams and bacon were smoked. A couple of milk cows were kept to produce fresh milk and butter for the family. Dock and Prince, the team of draft horses bought and trained on the Whitfill and Condor farms, were still the only source of power for farming the hilly fields.

Paul and Rosie were now planning for the future. Electricity would soon be extended west of the St. Paul community. They could make another attempt to bring water to the house. They could fix the mud road so that the car could be driven to the house in all weather.

The Beginning of the End

Rosie was now 38 years old. She would give birth to her tenth baby in December, 1952. For the first time in her married life she had experienced prenatal care. Since Grandma Janie's health was failing in old age, she could not attend the birth; and the young Doctor Nichols from Clarkson would come to their home. Pearl Clark, Tony Clark's wife would also attend the birth, guiding the doctor through the house and helping where needed.

Some of the children spent the night at Pearl's house and went to school the following day. Pearl had returned home and had told them that Rosie and the new baby were well. The baby girl had been named Anna Jean. Norma Howard, a teenage neighbor girl, was with Rosie, the baby, two year old Kathleen and four year old Christine at home.

When classes were dismissed in the afternoon, Norbert went to the ball diamond near the Darst's Store. Mr. Darst came outside and told him that Norma had come to the store a few minutes before to call the doctor and the ambulance. Rosie had lapsed into a coma.

Norbert ran all the way home, arriving about the time the ambulance arrived. Rosie was rushed to Saint Joseph Hospital in Louisville with Norbert sitting beside her in the ambulance holding baby Anna Jean. Paul, working the second shift at International Harvester, was notified that Rosie was on the way to the hospital and went directly there.

Rosie was still breathing slowly when they arrived at the hospital. The diagnosis was that Rosie had experienced a massive stroke caused by a blood clot. Within a few hours she died. Her body was carried to the Rogers Funeral Home in Clarkson, where it was prepared for burial, and then returned in the coffin to the farmhouse to spend a last day with the family.

The community was shocked. Rosie, one of the most friendly, healthy, responsible women in the community, could not be dead. She had survived nine previous childbirths with no problem. She was leaving behind eight children.

The traditional 24-hour vigil was started by the neighbors. The burial would be at the St. Paul Cemetery. At the funeral Mass, the Church was crowded. The pastor, Father DeNardi, in his eulogy tried to explain the human weakness in understanding God's plan, but nothing that he said could requite the sadness and sorrow of the family and the community.

14
THE LAST TEN YEARS

Life Goes On

Paul was faced with a major decision. Would he move the family to the city and continue to work at International Harvester? Would he quit the good job in the city and continue the farm operation as he and Rosie had planned 15 years earlier when the '37 flood had presented a similar decision point? Would he allow the younger children to live with relatives? Paul's sister Iva and her husband Carl had no children, and had asked that some of the children be allowed to live with them.

Paul's decision was immediate. He would keep the family together. He would sell the car to eliminate the debt. He would quit the job in the city and revitalize the farm operation. None of the children would be allowed to live with relatives.

His sisters who lived in the community and Rosie's mother volunteered to help when needed. Paul would be starting over again, a next phase of his many difficult experiences.

After the funeral and a trip to Louisville to quit his job in the factory, Paul immediately began work on incompleted fall projects around the farm. He advised the children that the best way to control their emotions was to stay busy. In quiet and serious discussions at mealtime, Paul emphasized that life had forever changed for the family. He also emphatically emphasized that the family would stay together and would survive.

The Farm Operation Renewed

The weather during the late summer and fall had been unusually dry. Because the hay crop had been light, the corn had been cut as fodder to feed the livestock during the winter. During the school vacation around the Christmas holidays, Paul and the boys hurried to gather the corn.

The corn fodder had been cut at knee-height and collected into shocks with the ears attached. The stalks from about eight rows of corn had been collected into a few rows of large shocks of fodder. Now the corn shocks were dismantled; the ears of corn pulled and hauled to the corn crib. The fodder was retied and collected near the barn. The ground was still so dry that dust could be kicked from the clods of soil.

As the shocks of fodder were dismantled, Paul and each boy selected a bundle from which he pulled the ears of corn. As they worked closely on their knees around the bundles of corn, the conversation turned to planning the farm crops for the next year. The boys suggested "more corn, more hogs, more money."

Paul was reluctant to agree to such a plan. "You boys are in school. I am the only worker. We have only one team of horses." Norbert, now a junior in high school answered, "I can quit school. We can rent more land. We can borrow a team from Grandpa Edward." Paul interrupted. Rising to his full height on his knees, he pointed his finger at Norbert. "You will not miss one day of school! End of conversation!"

Norbert knew that Paul blamed his own lack of education for many of the difficulties they had experienced. In past conversations he had pointed to the successful members of the community and attributed their success to their education. He had also pointed to the situations in which the difficulties were caused by the lack of education. So Norbert knew that the discussion was settled in favor of education.

Paul was projecting long-term into the future. It was as if he was saying: "Get an education. Move away from this God-forsaken place!" Since he'd been a young teenager, Paul had worked hard, struggling to survive without achieving success. With Rosie's death, he had reached the lowest point of his life.

Subsistence Farmer

The term "subsistence farmer" defined the next ten years of Paul's short and difficult life. His sister Iva provided the primary care for the family. She had time to help since she and Carl had no children. Rosie's mother, Mary Alta, who lived near Iva, also visited the family weekly. They cared for the children, cleaned and washed clothing and helped cook. Ann Mary and Mattie, Paul's other two sisters, visited and contributed as they were needed.

The older children were given additional responsibilities in the kitchen: cooking and washing dishes. Martina, now 11 years old, was elevated to the role of "mother." She cared for the babies and cooked meals when she was not in school. Her responsibilities were increased to a greater degree than those of her brothers and sisters.

Paul attempted to increase the farm operation, but the progress was slow. With little money available and additional family expenses, expansion was difficult. Additional heifers were grown into the herd. Additional brood sows were kept to increase the number of marketable hogs. Land was rented to grow more corn to feed the additional livestock. Dock and Prince, the old team of horses on which Paul had depended since living on the Whitfill farm, were still dependable. But how long they would be able to perform at this accelerated pace was questionable.

The progress that Rosie and Paul had imagined was at a standstill. Electricity had not been installed west of St. Paul Church and the dirt road was still impassible much of the year. Water was still carried from the spring under the hill and the cool spring was the only form of refrigeration during hot weather.

The windows were opened at night to let the cool breezes blow through the house. The family was lulled to sleep by the chirping of the crickets and the songs of the many bugs, the screech owls and the whippoorwills.

A New Team of Wild Mules

As the team of aging horses grew older and slower, Paul bought a team of large, mature but untrained mules from a retired farmer who had made no attempt to train them when they were young. They truly were like wild mules. Strangers were their enemies.

Paul bought long ropes to attach to their halters. This distance gave the mules a zone of comfort while they became acclimated to their new owner. With time and patience, the mules submitted to the training. When they were dependable as the primary work team, the old team of horses was sold.

The Family Matures

Because of Paul's emphasis on education, school was the one constant in the lives of the children. A couple of hours of homework after supper in the evening were routine. The battery radio was the only distraction. Every child was expected to complete their high school education.

As the older children finished high school they got jobs away from home or joined the army. Norbert got a job in a woodwork factory and completed an apprenticeship as a cabinet maker. Samuel joined the National Guard and trained for several months at Fort Sill, Oklahoma. Then he got a job at the Brown-Williamson cigarette factory. Daniel joined the Navy and was sent to Taiwan, which had recently seceded from China and its Communist form of government. Martina took a job at the Kelly Beehive Factory near Clarkson so she could live at home and help the younger children.

As the farm operation expanded and the older children left home, Paul bought a small farm tractor. The mules were still used to cultivate the hills on the old Langley farm.

Modern Technological Changes

Electrical lines were extended west of St. Paul Church in 1958 by the Rural Electrical Administration that supplied electricity to the end of the ridge in the Mount Hebron community.

Paul immediately had the house wired for electricity. Electric lights, a refrigerator and an electric cook stove were the first acquisitions. An electric washing machine, a used radio and a television followed. Water was still carried from the spring, however and the dirt road was still impassable for a few months each year. The children walked to school on a footpath that went through the adjoining farms.

At the age of 52, Paul was catching up with the technological world. Since being taken out of school in the sixth grade to support the family when his father's health had failed, he had experienced full responsibility for his parental family and for his own family with Rosie. His life had been a life of full responsibility and continuous manual labor. With the exception of a short bout of malaria and a serious burn as a teenager, his health had cooperated. But he knew that if he could pump water to the house and improve the dirt road, he could live much more comfortably.

Paul had survived the depression, the 1937 flood and Rosie's death. He had started his family during the Great Depression and had rented and reclaimed abandoned farms. He had moved with his young family into old log cabins built by the first settlers in the 19th century and abandoned them as modern structures were built. He had depended on the skills learned from his parents; skills on which they depended during the last half of the 19th century.

Another Sudden Death

Paul still provided the fiddle music for the square dances held in the school basement. He traded work with the neighboring farmers planting corn and baling hay. He was slowly adjusting to the advancements in technology and farming practices.

Everyone was surprised when Paul, an active member of the community, died suddenly of a stroke. Like Rosie's death, Paul's was sudden and unexpected. He was working long hours on the farm finishing the spring planting and setting out the tobacco plants.

During the night of June 1, 1964 he suffered convulsions and then lapsed into a coma. He was rushed by ambulance to St. Joseph Hospital in Louisville, the same hospital where Rosie had died. Within a few hours he had died of a massive stroke caused by a blood clot in the brain.

The family and community were in shock as they had been after Rosie's death. Paul had been sharing work and trading farm equipment with the neighborhood farmers the previous week. The

Catholic Church was again crowded for the funeral Mass. The eulogy concentrated on Paul's cooperation with the neighborhood farmers and his contribution within the parish. Father Powell repeated a conversation he had overheard between Paul and a neighbor. The neighbor had asked for Paul's help planting corn. Without hesitation, Paul's response was "Yes, I will help plant your corn." The priest also mentioned a conversation between himself and Paul discussing Paul's contribution in the parish by providing music for the weekly square dances. Paul's response was "As long as one person enjoys it, I will provide the music."

Paul was buried beside Rosie in the St. Paul Church Cemetery.

Completing Their Dreams

Rosie and Paul both died while trying to provide a comfortable home for a healthy, happy and educated family. Their lives ended before their dreams were fulfilled, but their idea of the importance of education and a strong work ethic provided the foundation from which their dreams were completed.

The younger children continued their education. Using the funds from the farm system that Paul had established, the old log house that had been built eighty years before was overhauled. The improvements included a modern kitchen, a dining room and two extra bedrooms. Water was finally pumped to the house from the spring under the steep hill, and plumbing was installed. From the two new porches and the large windows on three sides, the view over the hills and the forests was uninterrupted for miles.

The dirt road to the house was straightened, graded and graveled. The road, which had probably evolved from an old Indian trail crossing Meeting Creek at Tood's Ford, was now open for year-round travel.

Within a few years, the dreams that Paul and Rosie had worked to achieve during their married life were realized by their children. The success resulted from Paul and Rosie's hard work, their positive attitudes and their consideration and care for others. These were the qualities that they had learned from their parents and grandparents and passed on to their eight children.

More History
&
Geneology
of the
Clark and Milliner
Families

15
THE CLARK FAMILY COMES TO AMERICA

Sir George Calvert, a Roman Catholic in England, applied for a charter for land in Maryland in 1629. He died before the charter was granted. His sons received the charter and in 1633-34 organized an expedition to move settlers to the colony. Two ships, the Ark and the Dove, carried about 200 settlers, a mixture of Catholics and Protestants. One of the brothers, Leonard Calvert, established the first settlement of St. Mary's City on a river he named the St. Mary's River, that flowed past their landing spot into the Chesapeake Bay. He served as the English governor of the colony.

Shortly after the colony of St. Mary's was established, Robert Clark migrated to Maryland with a group of Jesuit Priests, the first of the Clarks to come to America from England. He was born in 1610 in England and died in 1664 in St. Mary's County in Maryland.

Robert worked as a surveyor. In 1652, 18 years after the Maryland settlement was established, Robert Clark's son, also named Robert, was born. These two Clark family generations lived and died in St. Mary's County.

The grandson of the original Robert was named Thomas Clark (1688-1740--different searches vary the dates) married Grace

Greenwell in 1709. Grace gave birth to 12 children, eight boys and four girls. This family lived and died in St. Mary's County. John Clark, 1724-1755, the son of Thomas and Grace, and his wife, Elanor Gough, were the fourth and last generation of Clarks to live their entire lives in St. Mary's County

About 150 years after the move from England to Maryland, in 1785, after the lands west of the Appalachian Mountains were taken by Americans from the English in the Revolutionary War, many Catholics, including Clark ancestors, moved to Kentucky.

John Clark's son, Richard Langhorne Clarke (1749-1814, married Chloe (last name unknown) and lived for about 20 years in Maryland. Five of Richard and Chloe's seven children were born there. The other two were born after their emigration to Kentucky.

At the beginning of Maryland's history, the Calvert founders of the Maryland Colony, had introduced religious freedom as part of the original Maryland charter. Then, in 1688, after 'The Glorious Revolution' in England, that religious openness ended. The central British government, which controlled the colonial governments, promoted the Anglican Religion as a state religion. By law, Catholics could not hold office, vote, or serve on juries. Under different governors, in many towns, over many years, Catholics were excluded as residents. In certain areas their churches were closed and Catholics were persecuted.*

During the Revolutionary War (1775-1783), the British Army and Navy controlled most of the area around Chesapeake Bay. The colonial population of families around the Bay suffered unbearably.

_____ * See "Maryland: Hardly a Refuge for Persecuted Catholics," by Brian Kelly, March 17, 2009. Posted at Catholicism.org.

The British soldiers lived by scavenging livestock from the farms and plundering the households. As a consequence of that property destruction, many people could not pay their bills and lost title to their property. These financial losses, combined with the inherent prejudices in the social system, were too much for many Catholic families, who decided after the war to move to the cheap (or free if a veteran) open lands in Kentucky.

Illinois, Indiana, Tennessee and Kentucky, all captured from England, had been opened for settlement and veterans of the war were paid with the lands in these states. Both George Washington and Thomas Jefferson were given land in Central Kentucky near the area where Richard and Chloe Clark settled with their five children. Richard and Chloe were part of an organized group of Catholic families who moved from Maryland to Kentucky. It is probable that Richard, a Patriot, was given free land.

When 60 Catholic families arranged to move as a group, Bishop Carroll of Baltimore promised to send a priest to minister to the group. In 1785, 25 more families moved to Kentucky. Their records show that they traveled overland to Pittsburg where they built flatboats for the trip down the Ohio River. After landing at what is today Maysville, Kentucky, they travelled another 150 miles through the wilderness to central Kentucky, settling around the area that is today Nelson County and its County Seat at Bardstown. As other families moved from Maryland to Kentucky, they rapidly spread into the adjoining counties of Marian, Hardin, Grayson, Washington and Breckinridge.

When they arrived in Kentucky with their family of five children, Richard Langhorne and Chloe Clark settled temporarily in Nelson County. Their oldest son, Wilford (1770-1815) born in Maryland, was married to Elizabeth Strader in 1792 in Nelson County. Shortly afterward, Richard moved his family from Nelson County to Breckinridge County, where he died in 1814. Wilford also moved his family to Breckinridge County (1810 census) and eventually into Grayson County where he died in 1815.

These moves were journeys of nearly 100 miles. Travel at that time was by ox cart through the wilderness, over Indian trails, fording rivers and creeks, through the shallow riffles. The trip would have taken several days and the threat of attack by cougars and bears was a constant worry. The possibility of an attack by a band of Indians was also still a threat. By contrast, their homes in Maryland had been in well established farming communities with churches, shops, towns, doctors and banks, but they had faced unbearable political/religious conditions.

Over many years, Bishop Carroll did send missionaries to Kentucky to minister to the rapidly expanding Catholic population. Father Whelan, the first missionary, stayed in Kentucky until 1790. In 1792, Father Rohan replaced Father Whalen and organized the construction of the first small log church at the site of today's town of Holy Cross, ten miles south of Bardstown.

The missionary who administered to the settlers for the longest period of time was Father Badin. He was ordained in 1793 in Baltimore, the first priest to be ordained in America. On horseback he visited Catholic families in half a dozen counties, distributing Communion, hearing confessions and administering the last rites to the sick and the dying.

As the Catholic settlements grew, Father Badin convinced Bishop Carroll to establish a Kentucky See, a Bishop's office of authority, at Bardstown in 1805. Several religious orders of priests and nuns moved into the area: Jesuits, Franciscans and Dominicans. They used the Kentucky monasteries as a base from which to send missionaries to the Northwest Territories. The Sisters of Charity established a convent at Nazareth near Bardstown about 1812. The Trappist monks established Gethsemane. The area around Bardstown is today known informally as "The Holy Land."

As the population of Catholic families continued to grow, another missionary, Father Nerinckx, saw the need to build several churches. In Grayson County two churches were built: St. Augustine in 1815 at Grayson Springs, and St. Paul, ten miles further west, in 1812. St. Mary of the Woods and St. Romuald, both in Breckinridge County, were built about the same time.

Although Richard Langhorn and his oldest son, Wilford, lived in Grayson and Breckinridge Counties when these churches were built, neither of their gravestones have been found. At that time, many of the graves were only marked with field stones.

Wilford continued as a family name in the Clark lineage until recent times. At the Clark-Milliner reunion in 2013, one of the Clark elders mentioned a young relative named Wilford. Records show that an earlier Wilford Clark (1845-1923) donated the land for the site of the St. Paul Church when it was moved from the cemetery to the present location.

The 19th century Wilford Clark's son, Matthew, born in 1814 in Grayson County, married Mary Mariah Bray. Their son, Charles Abraham Clark, was Paul Clark's grandfather. Charles Abraham married Mary Margaret Gray in 1861 shortly before the beginning of the Civil War. In less than a year, he was a soldier, training at Camp Wortham under his wife's father, Captain Anderson Gray. They were in the Union army, 27th Regiment of the Kentucky Infantry.

Camp Wortham at Grayson Springs was the training camp for hundreds of soldiers. Many were Charles Abraham's friends and relatives from Grayson, Hardin and Breckinridge Counties. In April, 1862, the 27th Regiment went to Shiloh in Tennessee to bury over

1,700 dead Union soldiers. They also buried wagon loads of amputated arms and legs, and they burned 5,000 dead horses.

The 27th regiment, in which Charles Abraham and his father-in-law Anderson Gray served, was primarily a work horse regiment defending railroad tracks and reconstructing railroad bridges destroyed by the Confederates. The railroad systems were necessary for supplying Union troops with munitions manufactured in the North. The regiment participated in the Battle of Perryville in Kentucky, pursuing Confederate General Braxton Bragg. The 27th Regiment also defended against the guerrillas under Confederate General John Hunt Morgan and participated in several battles in the South. Charles mustered out March 29, 1965. Both Charles Abraham and Captain Anderson Gray were buried in St. Paul Cemetery.Charles Abraham's son, Isaac Thomas Clark, 1866-1942, Paul's father was born, lived and died in Grayson County.

The ancestry of Ann Jane Langley (1876-1956), Isaac's wife, has not been researched beyond her third Great-Grandfather, Charles Langley (1799-1870), who was born in Kentucky. Jane's ancestors married into several family lines in the Grayson County community: Condors, Milners, Whitfills, Clarks and Burkheads. It is not clear whether they were members of the Catholic migration from Maryland or veterans of the Revolutionary War who were paid with lands in Kentucky. Her father, Charles Langley (1849-1923) built the dog-trot cabin and the log barn about 1880 on the farm that Rosie and Paul purchased in 1946. The log house had been overhauled but the log barn still existed in its original state when they moved there.

16
REMEMBRANCE:
IKE and JANIE CLARK

Piecing Together Grandpa Ike's Story

Ike and Janie's life-stories would fill an entire book, but it is impossible for us to know their complete stories. During the first half of their lives as a family, indications are that they lived comfortably in the top 25% of the rural society, both socially and economically.

Ike, born in 1866, (the gravestone is mismarked 1865) grew up during the Industrial Revolution. Most of Ike's working career was spent as a professional carpenter. He built wooden bridges and depots for the rapidly expanding railroad system. He built churches with steeples. He also built houses and barns in the community.

Ike's son Johnny, born in 1898, remembered "piles of chains, ropes and pulleys in the shed." He also remembered a miner's hat with an attached candle holder, the lighting system of miners before the introduction of the calcium carbide system to produce acetylene gas. Did he work in the mines when he was a young man?

Ike married when he was almost 30 years old. Farmers, 40 miles away in an adjoining county, remembered: "A couple of Clarks from Grayson County lived with us while building a large barn." Janie, in her later years, told her grandchildren about Ike "working with a local railroad engineer, Mr. Henry Darst, building wooden railroad bridges and depots." A house and barn built by Mr. Darst near St. Paul Church and School.are still functional.

Pictures of Ike exist, one probably taken before he was married, wearing an expensive suit with vest, tie, scarf and a gold watch fob with three medallions They exemplify his ambition as a young man during the industrial revolution. Another picture of Ike as a middle-aged man in a semi-formal business suit, symbolic of prosperity, gave credence to his self-confidence and accomplishments. Pictures of Janie as a beautiful, well groomed, older middle-aged woman wearing a fancy dress, a pearl necklace and a lace collar verify their status as elite members of the simple rural society.

Afterward, when fate reversed their progress, following years of failing health, a weak economy, a house fire, and more—they were reduced to the bottom 25 percent.

Catastrophes

Several major life changes happened within a few years. Ike's body, under the stress of hard manual labor, failed. Their house burned in the early 1920s, destroying everything except their night clothes. Ike's son Paul told stories of house parties and music parties held by his older brothers and sisters before this fire. They owned a phonograph and several musical instruments including an organ, but all of these were destroyed in the house fire.

At the same time, a post-war recession following WWI drastically reduced farm prices. The tobacco market, controlled by a buyer's monopoly, was temporarily destroyed. The family farm on which Ike and Janie depended after Ike's health failed was no longer a viable means of making a living.

With his broad experiences, Ike must surely have advised his older sons to move to a location with more opportunity. Lawrence and his wife moved to Richmond, Indiana where they raised his family. Johnny and Bernard with their wives soon followed.

Paul, born in 1912, was taken out of school in the sixth grade to help support the family. He, with his two younger brothers, Francis and David, struggled to dig a living from the worn-out hill farm until Ike died. They experimented with making whiskey, in great demand during prohibition. In the fall, apples from the orchard that Ike had planted when his body started to fail, were picked and sold.

After Paul and Rosie married in 1932, Paul's youngest brothers David and Frances still lived with Ike and Janie on the farm. In time Francis married and he and Mary Alpha moved to Louisville. David and Ann married in 1939 and continued to live on the farm until Ike died in October, 1942. Afterward, Janie lived alone in the farm house.

GRANDPA IKE

Born 'bout eighteen-sixty-five,

Through civil war the states survived;

Old Abe had won the war and freed the slaves,

Ike grew up a healthy man.

He travelled wide; he settled down.

Married young Janie; to her his love he gave

Ike helped his neighbors 'round the farm,

Built their houses, built their barns.

His children numbered nine, a fun-filled clan.

A railroad man, a poor boy's dream,

Built railroad bridges o'er the streams.

Ike helped to built the railroads 'cross this land.

When his body slowed and failed,

Ike no longer drove the nail,

His orchard grew, he sold the fruit for gain.

A wheelchair sat beside his bed,

A downy pillow 'neath his head,

White linens o'er his body soothed the pain.

The fruit trees bloom; the bobwhites sing.

The rhubarb grows come early spring.

Long Nancy rides side saddle down the lane.

They visit while sick Isaac rests,

Arrange for Ike soft feather beds,

Wife Janie cares for Ike who lives in pain.

When Ike's life came to an end,

A pine box built by neighbor, Jim,

Was lowered in the grave that mournful day

The leather straps that lowered it there

Were driving lines from the old grey mare.

Ike rests beneath that red Kentucky clay.

-Song by Norbert Clark

Grandma and Midwife: Ann Jane

Although Janie lived alone after Ike died, she had many visitors. The Clark family was always socially involved with the community, and Janie was a midwife who had been intimately involved with practically every person in the neighborhood. She helped deliver her own granddaughter, Darlene, the day before her husband Ike died. After Ike's death, many neighbors, Protestant and Catholic, visited Janie regularly.

In her later years, after Ike died, Janie was still an energetic, active manager. For example, while she was living alone on the farm, Paul and Rosie with their three children visited for the day. Janie was glad to see the family, even though they were unexpected. She immediately took control. "Paul, put your horses in the barn and feed them. Catch that old rooster by the barn; we will have chicken and dumplings. Rosie, take care of the children. Norbert, we will pick green beans and tomatoes and dig a few potatoes in the garden. And let's pick peaches for a cobbler! Paul you will need to cut more wood for the cook stove."

Two hours later, they sat down to a delicious dinner with happy chatter and gossip. To the children the atmosphere was that of a party. The chicken and dumplings from the pressure cooker, the fresh vegetables, and the dessert, all prepared with cooperation from everybody, was primarily the result of Janie's outgoing personality and her industrious nature. With no gas or electricity, no running water, no refrigeration, no grocery store, financially destitute, no government support system...at the age of about 65, she was totally self-reliant and productive, using skills learned in her childhood.

Grandma Janie Moves

Janie sold her farm at Mt. Hebron and moved back to her childhood home when Paul and Rosie bought the old Langley farm that had belonged to her parents. She lived independently in her one room, cooking much of her food and entertaining guests there.

Her most important contribution to Rosie and Paul's family was as a baby sitter. As the midwife in the Mt. Hebron community, Janie had a special attachment to the babies. She enjoyed rocking the babies, singing lullabies and ballads such as Rock-A-Bye Baby, Big Rock Candy Mountain, and The Ballad of Jessie James.

She enjoyed taking the older children fishing in Meeting Creek, where she had fished as a child. With homemade rigs tied to green poles cut from trees on the creek bank, they could usually catch enough sunfish, bluegills, rock bass and small perch for supper for the family.

With a bar of soap, a couple of wash cloths and a towel, under the pretense of going swimming, she sometimes supervised the Saturday bath for the children in a shallow pool in the spring branch or in the shallow riffle at Tood's Ford.

Grandma Janie understood the cycles of nature. She kept account of the phases of the moon and encouraged Paul to follow the traditions popular with farmers before the science of agriculture was understood. Paul's usual response to his mother's direction to plant in a certain phase of the moon was: "Mom, I'm not planting it on the moon."

Janie knew where the hazelnuts, the walnuts and the hickory nuts grew. She was the first in the spring to pick the wild greens: purslane, sorrel, dock, lambs quarter, plantains, and poke and wild onions. She could cook a tasty breakfast of lettuce, hot bacon grease, wild onions and scrambled eggs.

With the help of the children, Janie picked wild grapes in the fall. The grapes not used for a few cans of jelly were fermented with a generous supply of sugar for a couple of quarts of sweet wine. The rinds of the watermelons were processed into pickles or sweet preserves. She wasted nothing.

Going to the Doctor

As Janie's health weakened, she was encouraged by Paul and Rosie to go to the doctor, but she was very suspicious of his favorite prescription: morphine. A few members of the community had become addicted to the pain killer, experiencing serious long-term health problems. So Janie asked Paul to help her avoid being given morphine.

Paul took her to Dr. Phelps, the only general practitioner in Leitchfield. His practice was on a walk-in schedule. Janie was left to await her turn while Paul ran errands. When Paul returned to the office, Janie was ready to go home. The doctor had provided medicine, so back at home, Janie took the medicine and went to bed.

Later in the evening, a loud noise was heard in Janie's room. Paul and Rosie rushed to help. The room was filled with smoke and Janie was lying in the opposite corner of the room far from her bed. The stove was knocked out of position and the stovepipe had fallen. While Paul opened the windows, moved the stove into place and reinstalled the stovepipe, Rosie helped Janie into bed.

Janie told them that she had dreamed that she was a duckling walking on a bridge over a small stream. She decided to jump into the water for a swim. During that escapade, she had knocked the stove askew and fallen to the floor. Luckily, the fire in the stove had died down. Upon inspection, the medicine did turn out to be morphine, so Rosie threw it into the stove. Janie recuperated using the home remedies of smelly camphor and liniment.

Final Years

Janie lived with Paul and Rosie's family until her health started to fail. She visited her three sons and their families in Richmond, Indiana. She walked to daily Mass at St. Paul Church in all weather, summer and winter. An important part of the daily Mass experience was the social contact with her friends.

Several of the older farm couples and widows had sold their farms as they grew older. They built or rented houses in the St. Paul community near the church and the general store; most of them attended Mass daily. Afterward they talked with each other about their health, their gardens or the accomplishments of their children and grandchildren.

Janie, who had grown up in this community seventy years before had known most of these friends since childhood. After living most of her adult life in the Mount Hebron community, she was renewing her childhood friendships.

As her health declined and Paul's family grew, Janie moved to live her last few years with her daughter Ann Mary's family. Arthritis crippled her hands and caused her to be bent over. She died at age 80 in 1956, and is buried next to Ike at St. Francis Cemetery.

ANN JANE

Yoke the oxen; Hitch the sled,

Maple buds are turning red.

Maple sap drips slowly from the trees.

Hot sap boils above the fire,

Hot steam smells of maple syrup.

Young Janie tastes the maple syrup sweets.

Tote cool water in small pails.

Pick the wild greens from south hills.

Janie cooks brown cornbread; wild greens steam,

Dandelions and mouse-eared dock,

Green wild onions, stalks of poke,

Workmen eat the first wild greens of spring.

Fishing poles are green and long.

Shiny hooks are sharp and strong.

Happy children fishing in cool creeks,

If the moon is in the phase;

If earthworms are tasty bait;

Janie's skillet waits to cook fresh fish.

Play the fiddle; dance a jig

Slap the base; roast the pig.

The party starts; musicians start tp play

Pick that guitar; sing a song.

Chord the organ; hum along.

We'll sing and play until the break of day.

Storm clouds thunder in the night;

Holy candles burning bright;

Will lightning strike our humble home tonight?

Wake grandchildren from their beds;

"Pray the Rosiery; bow your heads."

Grandma Jane prays safety from God's might.

Fruit trees bloom; the bobwhites sing;

Rhubarb sprouts come early spring.

Long Nancy rides side-saddle down the lane.

They visit while sick Isaac rests;

Arrange for Ike soft feather beds;

Wife Janie cares for Ike who lives in pain.

-Song by Norbert Clark

17

MILLINER FAMILY HISTORY

Grandpa Ed, the Traditionalist

Rosie Milliner Clark's parents, Edward (1890-1965) and Mary Alta (1893-1973), repeated the lives of their ancestors, using the skills learned from their parents and grandparents.

The philosophy "Early to bed and early to rise makes a man healthy, wealthy and wise," was the main guide for Ed Milliner's life. He went to bed when the chickens went to roost at twilight. He awoke early in the morning before daylight. Using the lantern in the barn he fed the horses and harnessed them for work in the fields. He depended on his children to provide manual labor that was inherent in this survival mode of operation.

Ed had not gone to school and could neither read nor write. He used the tools and methods that his parents and grand-parents had used. He planted the old varieties of corn. He cut the corn fodder, ignoring the modern varieties of hay and the modern equipment for baling hay. He did not understand the science of fertilizers and lime in agriculture, preferring to farm the naturally fertile bottom lands. The annual renewal of the fertility in the soil by the flooding creeks assured a good yield with the use of little or no fertilizer. He would travel for miles to rent bottom land from neighboring farmers. The extra labor required by this arrangement was provided by his four healthy sons.

One of Ed's skills was raising and training horses and mules. Rosie, their oldest daughter, told a story about his ability to train unmanageable mules. He bought at auction a mule considered untrainable by its owner. He paid twenty five dollars for the large, red, mean mule. A year later he sold the trained mule for three hundred dollars. Ed had trained the unmanageable mule by hitching it between trained mules when he was working in the woods, harvesting logs for lumber to build a house.

After moving into a small log cabin on the Milliner farm when he and Mary Alta were married, Ed built a larger house as their family grew. He split white oak shakes with a froe and mallet for roofs for the house, the large barn and the out buildings.

When Ed's two oldest daughters, Rosie and Theresa, married and started their families, they visited on the weekend with the grandchildren. Sunday dinner at Grandpa Ed's house was an interesting experience for grandchildren studying English and grammar in school. Ed used the old English versions of verbs such as 'hered' and 'seed' for 'heard' and 'saw'. No one corrected Grandpa. His flawless table manners, tracing back several generations, were unique.

"Grandpa, would you like more beans?"

"If you please...If you please."

Or, when Ed started to pass a bowl around the table, "Once around, once around!" His memorized version of the Grace before meals was recited at record-setting pace with his hands folded and his head bowed. He diligently fulfilled his duties as a parent and grandparent with his ancient versions of table manners and grace before meals.

Ed's energy and survival skills provided financial stability for the family through the farm depression of the 1920s and the financial depression of the 1930s. His older children in their later years bragged about Ed's ability to survive independently during the depressions. He did not apply for any of the government programs. Daily, life continued at the same traditional standards whether in or out of the depressions.

Grandpa Edward

Refrain

It was on that glorious morn

When my Grandpa Ed was born,

The little boy crawled out the cabin door.

He rode his mule to town; pick 'em up; set 'em down,

On his journey through this life forever more.

He could not read; he could not write;

Times were good and he was bright;

He learned to split the rail and plant the corn.

Built a house upon the hill; in the woods a little still

He raised a family counting eight and one.

When sorghum cane grew tall,

Leaves turned colors in the fall,

The smokehouse ever filled with country ham

Hot corn bread and black eyed peas,

"Once around," and, "If you please."

Country butter, apple pie, and candied yams.

Hearts were sad that dreadful day

Grandpa's sons were called away

Around the world to fight those wicked wars.

"Can this bloody war be won?"

"Where is God? Where are my sons?"

His mind forever more was filled with scorn.

His hair turned gray; his eyes grew dim;

Angels sang – sweet seraphim.

His life on earth did slowly drift away.

Will he learn to read up there,

Ride the mule and plow the furrow

As we recall his life on earth today?

-Song by Norbert Clark

208

Granny, the Worker

Mary Alta worked equally hard as her husband Edward. She gave birth to nine children: four boys and five girls. She raised a large garden, growing all the food for the family. She preserved, canned, pickled or dried food for the entire year. From a few milk cows, she churned butter and provided milk for the family. She set several brooding hens to grow fryers and a flock of laying hens and managed a large flock of geese that provided eggs and meat. She picked the goose down annually to fill pillows and feather beds. She sewed the family's dresses, shirts and underclothes. Mary Alta also taught these basic skills to the children.

In addition to caring for the garden, the kitchen, the chickens and the geese, Mary Alta took pride in her flowers. Certain varieties of the flowers were considered important to attract or repel insects from the garden plants. With the help of Ed and the boys, she installed houses for purple martins and house wrens, birds that were aggressive in controlling mosquitoes and insects around the house and garden.

The many varieties of flowers were cultivated with the same attention given the garden plants. The flowers, both annuals and perennials around the yard fence and the foundation of the house, bloomed continuously from early spring to late fall. The yard around the house was fenced with a white picket fence that protected the flowers from the chickens and geese. And the flowers did not end with the arrival of cold weather. Many of the plants were transferred into pots where they continued to thrive with the house plants through the winter.

Like most families of the time, Ed and Mary Alta planted a large orchard. With the June apples of early summer, the sweet apples in middle summer, the Sheepnose and the Maiden Blush in early fall, the

Winesaps and the Ben Davis in the late fall and winter, apples were a staple in the family diet. Canned and the dried apples extended the supply of apples throughout the year. One delicacy was fried apple pies made with dried apples.

While Ed considered work-skills of primary importance, Mary Alta valued education. She had completed the eighth grade at the Johnson Public School in the school house holler near her girlhood home, and she sent her children to the same Johnson school house, now moved to Salt River Road. Her three younger children were sent to St. Paul Parochial School where they finished high school. In her later years, Mary Alta read incessantly, late into the night.

Granny Was a Worker

Refrain:

Granny was a worker, Do Si Do

Granny went to heaven a long time ago.

Granny was an angel, fiddle De Dee

An angel up in heaven, there praying for me.

Granny in the garden Granny in the rain,

Granny in the smoke house, Granny down the lane,

Granny fed the chickens, the pigs in the pen;

Granny gathered eggs from the geese and the hens.

Granny milked the cow on a one-legged stool,

Granny raised the kids; sent the kids to school.

Granny read her books into the night;

She awoke in the morning before daylight.

Granny baked the corn bread, granny cooked the beans.

Granny fried the ham, the fat and the lean.

Granny baked the biscuits, the dried apple pies.

Granny churned the butter, that melts in your mouth.

Granny planted flowers 'round the garden fence.

Granny sewed her dress just to save a pence,

Granny said her prayers while on the run.

The Lord looked down, said, "Son of a gun!"

The Lord looked down, said "Granny, slow down!"

Granny said "Lord, I have to go to town.

Have to pay them taxes and the mortgage too,

Sew a new dress before I go with you."

The Lord said, "Granny, it's time to go."

Granny said "Lord, the answer is NO!

We have to strip tobacco; fix the barn door latch;

Set the hens so the eggs will hatch."

REFRAIN

-Song by Norbert Clark

Family Tragedies

Like all large families, Ed and Mary Alta's family was beset by several tragedies. Ed's ancestors had made whiskey, legally, before prohibition; he continued to make whiskey, illegally, during prohibition. The quality of his whiskey was exceptional and in great demand. Ed hired extra help to keep his still in operation twenty-four-hours-a-day.

Many of the men who had left the farm for the cities knew of the quality of Ed's whiskey. They bootlegged the whiskey to the clubs in the cities. One bootlegger posed as a door-to-door egg salesman in the large city of Louisville. He hid bottles of whiskey in an egg basket under a few eggs.

The illegal whiskey operation resulted in the arrest of their son, Andrew William. After spending a year in the county jail as punishment for his first offense, Andy continued making whiskey. He was arrested a second time and sentenced to two years in the federal prison at Eddyville.

The whiskey operation caused animosity among the neighbors. Husbands who tended to binge drink had convenient access to the illegal whiskey. Teenage boys experimented with the whiskey and a few became addicted. The wives and mothers in the community threatened and, in some cases, informed the sheriff about the illegal operation.

The pressure caused by the uncertainty of the illegal still caused Ed to experience a nervous breakdown. His belligerent and destructive behavior resulted in a trail at which the Judge interpreted his behavior as caused by a mental problem. He was released to home care as an alternative to going to the insane asylum.

Ed did recover and continued his traditional farming practices, while scaling down his whiskey making operation. However, two of his sons, Andrew William and Sylvester Herbert, who were both binge drinkers, were each killed in car wrecks while drinking. They both had survived four years fighting in WWII, but died as a result of alcoholism.

Another tragedy occurred when their son Joseph Edward (Joe Ed) was killed by a car while walking on highway 62 with a group of friends by Big Clifty. He had not been drafted into the army, possibly because of a crippled hand that had been damaged by a cross cut saw. Joe Ed had been Ed's primary helper when Andy and Herbert were in the army.

Joe Ed's sister, Rosie, experienced a premonition of her brother's death. She had repaired his hand when he was injured as a child. Rosie was taking a nap with her baby when she was suddenly awakened with a strong sensation that a terrible accident had happened. She rushed to the yard to check on her children , but found them all safe and playing happily. Confused and still disturbed, she returned to the house with the baby. Within the hour a neighbor came to tell Rosie that Joe Ed had been killed. He had died at the same time that Rosie had been awakened. Was it possible that he had turned to Rosie for comfort as he died?

Ed blamed the advancement of industry for his son's death: "Too many cars ---the damned dog wagons!" Shortly before he was killed, Joe Ed had split white-oak shakes with the froe and mallet to replace the old shakes on the large barn. He was continuing Ed's idea of living the traditional ways.

Why his two oldest sons were drafted into the army during WWII, Ed could not understand. He could not read and so was not familiar with the world history and politics responsible for the war.

His lack of education and travel restricted his understanding of the world to the small rural community where he was born and raised. The farm where he lived was part of the original land grant to his ancestors who fought in the Revolutionary War.

Ed did not own a radio and was not familiar with Nazism or Hitler's rise in Germany. Japan, Italy, Pearl Harbor and the South Pacific were fairy lands, outside of his comprehension. He questioned the sanity of a president who would send his sons and the neighborhood boys into war where many would be killed. He questioned the existence of a God who would permit such savagery. He blamed the advancement of military technology for the problems. In his comprehension, if people would "mind their own business and live the simple life" that he lived, there would be no wars.

When Ed's two oldest sons, Andrew and Herbert, half of his work force, were drafted into the army during WWII, both the immediate and the long term consequences were devastating. Ed's simple way of life was rapidly coming to an end.

After Ed died, Mary Alta, like many widows, sold the farm and built a house near St. Paul Church. She still maintained a large garden, canning and preserving the produce. Flowers were still an important part of her house, garden and life. Mary Alta valued the friendships of the several women with whom she attended daily Mass.

When Mary Alta died in 1973 at age 80, their place in history was remembered by their children and grandchildren.

18

Milliner Family Migration to Kentucky

Tracing the Milliner ancestry (also spelled Milner) has been difficult. Both Edward and Mary Alta were Milliners. Mary Alta's ancestry somewhat parallels that of the Clarks as members of the earliest settlers in central Kentucky about the time of the Revolutionary War.

Her mother, Marcella Whitfield's (later spelled 'Whitfill') ancestor, Christian Gutknect (1721-1781) was born in Germany and died in Kentucky. Christian and two of his brothers, Hans Michael and George, migrated from Germany to the British Colony of North Carolina in the mid-1700s. Upon arrival they changed their name to the English spelling, 'Goodnight'.

As some of the earliest American settlers in Kentucky, the Goodnight brothers experienced devastating harassment by the Indians and two were killed. Accounts attributed to their descendents described the attack in which Hans was scalped and killed and his son was wounded while they were on a journey from their previous home in North Carolina to Mercer County, Kentucky in 1781. His wife escaped and was found several days later hiding in the woods, almost dead.

In his Proclamation of 1763, King George III had forbidden English settlements west of the Appalachian Mountains. The Indians, in cooperation with the British in Canada and the Great Lakes, were enforcing this proclamation. The Indian attacks reached their peak in 1777 as they realized settlers were building permanent settlements.

George Goodnight was killed in 1780 when the Indians, again supported by the British from Canada, attacked Ruddel's Station in central Kentucky. Five of his children were captured by the Indians and his daughter Elizabeth gave birth to two sons by an Indian brave before she returned to her family at age 22.

The Goodnight's and Mary Alta's Milner ancestors connected when the great granddaughter of Hans Michael Goodnight, Marthena Conder (1807-1858), married William Milner (1805-1899) in Grayson County, Kentucky. Her father, George Conder (1745-1799) was born in Mecklenburg County, North Carolina and died in Washington County, Kentucky.

North Carolina was the first American colony to declare independence from the King of England. The council in Mecklenburg County wrote their own Declaration of Independence and implemented plans to join the other colonies in revolting against Britain.

The ancestry of Mary Alta's Milners has not been researched prior to this time. William and Marthena's son, James Milner (1833-1864) married Sarah Ellen Burkhead (1834-1906). She gave birth to six children before he was drafted into the Union Army as a Private, CompanyH, 4th KY Infantry on May 5, 1864.

He was taken prisoner by the Confederates during the Battle of Lovejoy station, September 2-6, at Jonesboro, Georgia. Held prisoner

217

at Charleston, South Carolina, he was paroled Dec. 10, 1864 and died the same day of chronic diarrhea.

Their son, William Riley Milner (1855-1936) married Marcella (Marty) Whitfill (1858-1951), Mary Alta's mother and Rosie's grandmother. Riley and Marty were the last generation to use the name Milner. Their children changed the spelling of the name to Milliner. The same change was recorded in the Edward Milliner Ancestry in the late 1800s.

Neither Mary Alta nor Edward's ancestry as Milners has been connected to a country in Europe. Family legends handed down from Mary Alta to Rosie described their line of Milners as "Black Irish" (the dark complected Irish). Mary Alta's complexion was quite dark. They were thought to have been descendents of the sailors in the Spanish Armada who were stranded in the villages on the shores of Northern Ireland after their ships were destroyed by the English Navy and the rough North Sea. Mary Alta talked with a crisp voice and a literate vocabulary that could have been interpreted as an Irish brogue. She did not develop the southern drawl traditional to many Kentuckians.

The ancestry of Edward Lorenzo Milliner (1870-1965), Rosie's father, is more uncertain. One record shows that William Milner (no dates) was born in Virginia. Both William and his son, Andrew Milner (1807-1884) are listed in the 1830 census as living in Grayson County, Kentucky. Andrew and his wife, Martha (1800-1878) were buried in the Catholic cemetery at St. Augustine Church. They would have lived in the community where Fr. Nerincky built one of the first Catholic Churches in Grayson County.

The son of Andrew Milner, James Sylvester Milner (1827-1862), married Mary Matilda Langley (1831-1905). She gave birth to six children before he was drafted into the Union Army in October, 1861. He was in Company A, 27th KY infantry with Captain Anderson Gray and Private Charles Abraham Clark, both ancestors of Paul Clark. Because he contacted tuberculosis, he was admitted to the General Hospital in Louisville and was discharged as a sergeant on July 9, 1862. He came home, died three weeks later, and was buried in St. Augustine Catholic Cemetery near Grayson Springs, Kentucky.

His wife Mary applied for a pension based on the claim that Sylvester contracted tuberculosis in the military. Several of their neighbors, including two doctors and the midwife for their six children, testified that "he had been healthy before joining the army and his widow and the children are very needy." Mary, the neighbors and the midwife signed their testimonies with an "X". Survival evidently took priority over education in the community at that time.

Isaac Milner, Rosie's fourth great grandfather in her mother Mary Alta's line of Milner ancesters, was granted two parcels of land on Meeting Creek and Rough Creek in 1821. Rosie was born and raised on the farm that family tradition claims to be one of the land grants on Meeting Creek. The farm is currently owned by Rosie and Paul's son, Daniel Clark.

Although the Milliners/Milners were Catholics who migrated to the open lands in Kentucky after the American Revolution, they were not members of the Catholic Migration from Maryland.

Bibliography

Lee, Dan. *Your Son until Death*, 2007.

Colins, Louis. *History of Kentucky*, 1878.

Webb, Benedict Joseph. *The Centenary of Catholicity in Kentucky*, 1884.

Ancestry.com, "The Kentucky Land Grants"

Ancestry.com, "Kentucky Marriages."

Aardvark_U.com/~E. Hayden/MCF/Maryland.HTM

www.fold3.com/image

Goodnight, S. H. *The Good(k)night (Gutknect) Family in America*, 1936.

The Encyclopedia Americana, International Edition, Volumes 16 and 18, 1968.

Author Note

Norbert Clark, the oldest son of Paul and Rosie Clark, moved back to the remote farm and continued their efforts after both his parents died at an early age. He took on the responsibility of being the legal guardian for his teenage brother and three teenage sisters still at home on the farm, emphasizing education for the younger children.

Both Samuel Clark and Martina Clark moved their young families back to the community so they could help Norbert with his efforts. The old house and the road were modernized and, building on the foundation that Rosie and Paul had struggled to establish in their 14 years as sharecroppers, the family completed the task.

Norbert continued his education and then worked as a chemical laboratory technician in research and development for 35 years. Short visits to the old farms where his parents struggled–most had been abandoned--provided a strong incentive to write this book. Because of the 1937 flood and the Great Depression, his parents experienced a reversal of financial progress and were forced to depend on survival skills honed by farmers in the 1800s. Growing up in that situation and living into the 21st century, Norbert Clark experienced life-styles of three centuries. Norbert and his wife Karen make their home in Freeland, Michigan.

Norbert Clark

Made in the USA
Lexington, KY
08 January 2015